STUDYING NATIONAL CREATIVITY

Abundance Or Scarcity

China, Byzantium, Arab World, Venice,
Egypt, Greece, Rome, Western World

William A. Therivel

Kirk House Publishers
Minneapolis, Minnesota

STUDYING NATIONAL CREATIVITY
Abundance Or Scarcity

China, Byzantium, Arab World, Venice,
Egypt, Greece, Rome, Western World

by William A. Therivel

Copyright © 2014 William A. Therivel. All rights reserved, including the right of reproduction in whole or in part, in any form.

Cover art: Early sixteenth century woodcut.

Library of Congress Cataloging-in-Publication Data

Therivel, William A., 1928-
  Studying national creativity : abundance or scarcity : China, Byzantium, Arab world, Venice, Egypt, Greece, Rome, western world / William A. Therivel.
    p. cm.
  Includes bibliographical references and index.
  ISBN-13: 978-1-933794-69-3
  ISBN-10: 1-933794-69-0
  1. Personality and creative ability. I. Title.
    BF698.09.C74T484 2014
    153.4—dc23

Kirk House Publishers, P.O. Box 390759, Minneapolis, MN 55439
www.kirkhouse.com
Manufactured in the United States of America

To Brigitte and Silvia

Contents

Preface 7

Introduction 9

1. Solving the Enigma of the Decline and Fall
   of Creativity in Imperial China 11

2. Solving the Enigma of the Constant Low Creativity
   of Imperial Byzantium 26

3. Solving the Enigma of the Decline of Creativity
   in the Arab World 33

4. Why Did Venice Have No Great Writers When
   It Had Great Painters, Architects and Musicians? 44

5. The Nile Made the Pharaonic UP Polytheism—
   the Sea the Greek DP Polytheism 53

6. The Decline and Fall of the Roman Empire 64

7. The DP Origins of Western Science 72

8. Conclusions 90

References 98

Author Index 106

Subject Index 108

Preface

Acknowledgment: My wife Brigitte and daughter Silvia helped me patiently with this book and it is to them that the book is dedicated.

References and footnotes follow the APA system which separates the references (at the end of the book) from the footnotes (at the bottom of each pertaining page). The separation allows for substantive footnotes that are completely devoted to expanding and clarifying the main text. If at all possible, I would ask the reader not to skip the footnotes.

To allow the reader a direct contact with the sources, most quotes are reported verbatim and not paraphrased. I use the quotes as quality bricks, or first class prefabricated sections, requiring no change on my part.

Whenever possible I have used existing translations of foreign texts; otherwise the translation is mine.

Introduction

China: Why did China fail to sustain its technological supremacy; why did it fail to develop modern science; and why did it even forget many of its discoveries and inventions? Joseph Needham, the great scholar of the history of Chinese science and technology, called it the "sixty-four thousand dollar question," and Joel Mokyr called it "the greatest enigma in the history of technology."

Byzantium: "The Byzantines preserved the cultural heritage of ancient Greece but scarcely developed it further" (H. W. Hausig). "Byzantine literature as a whole is not great literature; few would study it for pleasure" (Marshall & Mavrogordato).

Arab World: *What Went Wrong? - The clash between Islam and modernity in the Middle East;The Crisis of Islam*, and *The Crisis of Islamic Civilization* are the titles of three recent books (2002, 2003, 2009), the first two by Bernard Lewis, the third by Ali A. Allawi, formerly Minister of Defense and Minister of Finance in the Iraqi postwar government.

Venice: "In the fourteenth century, for reasons that no historian has fathomed, Florence—why not bigger and more powerful Venice?—took the vanguard of the peninsula's high cultural awakening, particularly in literature and the visual arts, remaining there until the sixteenth century" (Lauro Martines).

Egypt and Greece: Can geography help us understand the difference between the Egyptian UP polytheism and Greek DP polytheism, and the decline and fall of ancient Egypt?

Rome: "The causes and consequences of the fall of the Roman Empire in the West have been inexhaustible subjects of speculation and argument" (Norman Cantor, echoing Edward Gibbon's *The Decline and Fall of the Roman Empire)*.

Western World: Why was science born there, and not elsewhere?

Answering these questions is the aim of this book.

Each case is different, and will be treated differently. Yet, the analysis of one will resonate with the others, giving evidence for the fundamental importance of the nature of power (division of power or unity of power) for national character and creativity (birth and growth, decline and fall). The sequence of the chapters is not historical but ideological in moving toward the more complex cases and finally to the origins of the present world, with emphasis on the origins of Western science.

1

Solving the Enigma of the Decline and Fall of Creativity in Imperial China

1. The Sixty-Four Thousand Dollar Question

Why did China fail to sustain its technological supremacy; why did it fail to develop modern science; and why did it even forget many of its discoveries and inventions? Joseph Needham, the great scholar of the history of Chinese science and technology, called it the "sixty-four thousand dollar question" (1998, p. 7), and Joel Mokyr called it "the greatest enigma in the history of technology" (1990, p. 209).

> As explained by Robert Temple:
>
> One of the greatest untold secrets of history is that the "modern world" in which we live is a unique synthesis of Chinese and Western ingredients. Possibly more than half of the basic inventions and discoveries upon which the 'modern world' rests come from China. And yet few people know this. Why? The Chinese themselves are as ignorant of this fact as Westerners. From the seventeenth century onwards, the Chinese became increasingly dazzled by European technological expertise, having experienced a period of amnesia regarding their own achievements. When the Chinese were shown a mechanical clock by Jesuit missionaries, they were awestruck. They had forgotten that it was they who had invented mechanical clocks in the first place!
>
> It is just as much a surprise for the Chinese as for Westerners to realize that *modern* agriculture, *modern* shipping,

the *modern* oil industry, *modern* astronomical observatories, *modern* music, decimal mathematics, paper money, umbrellas, fishing reels, wheelbarrows, multi-stage rockets, guns, underwater mines, poison gas, parachutes, hot-air balloons, manned flight, brandy, whisky, the game of chess, printing, and even the essential design of the steam engine, all came from China.

Without the importation from China of nautical and navigational improvements such as ships' rudders, the compass and multiple masts, the great European Voyages of Discovery could never have been undertaken. Columbus would not have sailed to America, and Europeans would never have established colonial empires. Without the importation from China of the stirrup, to enable them to stay on horseback, knights of old would never have ridden in their shining armor to aid damsels in distress; there would have been no Age of Chivalry (1998, p. 9)

2. The Decline and Fall of Scientific-Technological Creativity

Creativity began to decline from the 3rd century AD, and almost halted in the 13th century: "China's lack of progress after 1400 is striking," wrote Mokyr, "not only in light of Europe's success, but also compared with its own performance in the previous centuries" (1990, p. 223).

The decline and fall of scientific-technological creativity (i.e., in agriculture, astronomy and cartography, engineering, domestic and industrial technology, medicine and health, mathematics, magnetism, physical sciences, transport and exploration, sound and music, and warfare) is evident from the tables of Temple's *The Genius of China: 3,000 Years of Science, Discovery and Invention* (1998). The list details 53 inventions and discoveries from 6th BC to 2nd AD (8 centuries); 38 in the subsequent eight centuries, and only 15 inventions and discoveries for the last eight centuries, from the 11th to the 18th. The final decline is even more evident if we look at the number of inventions and discoveries per century of the last period: 6 in the 11th century, then 2, 4, 2, none, 1 in the 16th century, then no more. And even that one discovery in the 16th century, of the equal temperaments in music, is less globally influential than previous ones.

3. **From *Quasi-Visitors* to *Insulars*[1]**

There have been many scholarly attempts to explain the decline and fall of Chinese creativity, but none of them have been convincing, due to the lack of attention to the gradual downgrading of the Chinese ethnopsychology from *quasi-visitorship* to ever stronger levels of *insularity*, under the impact of the imperial *unity of power* (actual and ideological).

In chapter 8, the *insular* mentality can be illustrated with the following comments, on the contemporary tripartite division of all social relations among the Chinese by professor Yang Kuo-shu, as reported by Kleinman and Kleinman (1991):

> The nearest compartment is occupied by family and close friends. Here, trust is unconditional, and certain private feelings can be revealed. The second compartment contains distant family and friends. Here trust is conditional, and feelings will only occasionally be expressed, and always with great caution. The most distant compartment contains relations with strangers. Here there is an absolute lack of trust, and inner experience is not to be expressed lest it is used against one's family and social network.... Demonstrating strong feelings, includingthe menaced and aggrieved affects of suffering, is dangerous, because it gives others power over relationships and restricts one's flexibility to respond effectively. Ultimately, uncontrolled emotional displays threaten one's position in a world of power. (p. 288)

These are the *insular* ways of thinking and life strategies of most Chinese in a country where formerly the emperor, and now the Communist Party, had undisputed power. Furthermore, these ways of thinking prevent new creativity and even erase the invention of previous centuries. However, *insularity* per se, cannot fully answer the "sixty-four thousand dollar question." The answer must include a discussion of footbinding and castration, and the ever increasing Unity of Power of the Chinese emperors that reach every corner of the empire through their learned bureaucrats, the mandarins.

---

[1] *Visitors,* raised under division of power, are independent, self-directed, confident, critical thinkers. They are creative. *Insulars,* raised under unity of power, are dependent, conformist, and intolerant of nonconformists, centered on family or clan. They are less creative.

4. The Main Contributor to the Extinction of Creativity: Footbinding

Footbinding is the horrible practice of drastically reducing the size of a girl's feet by deforming them with tight bandaging during her formative growth years, from age six to twelve. Requiring several months of relentless pressure, the binding cloths break the arch of the foot and force it upward in a bow so that the flat of the heel and the ball of the foot, which had formerly been horizontal, become perpendicular, in an artfully-produced lily of three or four inches. "In the beginning, it was a fashion developed by court dancers who performed on carved lotus flowers or carpets with lotus flower designs. Court circles and the upper class imitated the fashion, and it soon became a status symbol. In the course of the following centuries, the middle and even the lower classes imitated the upper-class fashion.... Footbinding which had been infrequent until the end of the eleventh century[2], became afterwards so widely imitated that people were ashamed not to practice it" (Levy, 1966, pp. 17, 40).

A 1929 study of women in Tinghsien, a rural area 125 miles south of Beijing, shows the extent of footbinding by age groups, among 1,736 females from 515 families.

Tinghsien Females With Bound and Unbound Feet, 515 Families, 1929

Age Groups	Unbound Feet	Bound Feet	Total	Percent Bound
Under 5	294	—	294	—
5-9	169	—	169	—
10-14	152	9	161	5.6
15-19	120	29	149	19.5
20-24	52	77	129	59.7
25-29	24	106	130	81.5
30-34	6	97	103	94.1
35-39	6	103	109	94.5
40 and over	4	488	492	99.2

(quoted by Levy, 1966, p.91)

---

[2] The 11th is the last century with a high number of inventions (6), in the Temple tables.

These figures point to a tragic near total prevalence of footbindingamong those born before 1890 confirmed by the eminent historian John K. Fairbank:

> When my wife and I lived in Beijing for four years in the early 1930s, three things impressed us as unusual. . . .Third, all women of middle age or over had bound feet, stumping about awkwardly on their heels as though the front sections of their feet had been amputated. Traveling in the countryside of five North China provinces, we never met a farmer's wife over the age of 30 whose feet were not bound.... The cruelest aspect of footbinding was that the peasant masses among the Chinese imitated the upper class. . . Apparently the custom was maintained in some areas but not in others. But binding was a widespread practice in the nineteenth century, and its effects were still visible in the 1930s.
>
> What was the psychic and social, to say nothing of the economic, cost of footbinding? Village women accepted it like the pains of childbirth and ridiculed anyone with normal feet. Did they believe the male theory that footbinding produced muscles that increased a husband's enjoyment of copulation? In mutilating themselves did they suffer any loss of self-respect, of self-confidence?. . . In the end could a bound-foot woman feel anything but inferior? a victim of remorseless fate? fearful of breaking convention? The trauma, conscious or unconscious, must have become part of the personality of Chinese women. (Fairbank & Goldman, pp. 173, 175-76).

In a prior article of 1990, Fairbank wrote:

> This excruciating practice, which darkened the lives of probably more than half of the women in China in recent centuries, is today generally ignored. No doubt we China specialists love our China and hate to make it seem sordid. Only this, I think, can account for the neglect of a social custom carried out by women ostensibly to please the men but with incalculable psychic consequences. Once your feet were bound they were with you night and day, a source of pain and weakness impossible to eliminate and constantly proof of your inferiority" (p. 17).

In the same vein, Hong (1997) wrote:

> In Chinese history until the recent past women's bodies have been the focus of their humiliations, exploitation and oppression. This is irrefutable. It is through their bodies that they have been subjected both physically and psychologically: first and foremost through the institution of footbinding—a brilliant and brutal instrument of control. Women unable to walk adequately were easy to restrain. Furthermore, the intense physical suffering brought about by the process of breaking and binding the feet in early childhood produced a passivity, stoicism and fatalism that effectively 'bound' not only the feet but also the mind and the emotions." (p. 289)

Then, as narrated by Second Sister Chang Yu-i, to her niece Chang Pang-Mei:

> Of the four girls in the family, I was the one who cared the most about education, even from the very beginning. First Sister only cared about pleasing people and playing mah-jongg; later on, she became addicted to opium.... I think my desire for education was due to the fact that I knew that I had been born into changing times. Also, I admired my Second and Fourth Brothers very much. And I was the first in my family among the girls not to have bound feet. First Sister, who was only two years older than I, had bound feet but absolutely no patience for books and learning.... When [in 1912] we reached the campus of the school, First Sister groaned. "It's so big," she said. Her feet were bound. "How am I going to walk around here?" First sister and I were put in the same room on the second floor of the dormitory building. We shared it with four other girls, three of whom also had bound feet like First Sister. The four of them were always complaining about the size of the campus, which I thought was actually very small. There were only three buildings: the dormitory, the classroom, and the dining hall.... Unlike First Sister, I worked hard. Only one other student at school studied as hard as I. This girl had normal feet too. (Chang, 1997, pp. 56-60)

A contributing cause to the footbinding of women was that the men were losing command over their lives and were becoming soft:

Footbinding was an alteration of the body that changed everything about a woman's physical being. She would move about less, sitting rather than standing, staying home rather than going out. With less exercise, she would be softer, more languid. From poetry, we know of men's attraction to languid women, especially unhappy beauties longing for absent men. For women to be smaller, softer, more stationary, and more languid would of course enhance the image of men as larger, harder, more active. Because the ideal upper-class man was by Sung times [960-1279 AD] a relatively subdued and refined figure[3], he might seem effeminate unless women could be made even more delicate, reticent, and stationary. (Ebrey, 1993, p. 41)

Even as recently as 1915 (footbinding was officially banned in 1902, and only completely discontinued about 1919), a Chinese author, explained "the psychological advantages" which footbinding brought to the Chinese male:

The bound foot is the condition of a life of dignity for man, of contentment for woman. Let me make this clear. I am a Chinese fairly typical of my class. I poured too much over classic texts in my youth and dimmed my eyes, narrowed my chest, crooked my back. My memory is not strong, and in an old civilization there is a vast deal to learn before you can know anything. Accordingly among scholars I cut a poor figure. I am timid, and my voice plays me false in gatherings of men. But to my footbound wife, confined for life to her house except when I bear her in my arms to her palanquin, my stride is heroic, my voice is that of a roaring lion, my wisdom is of the sages. To her I am the world; I am life itself. (quoted by Levy, 1966, pp. 88-89)

However, this hobbled woman with bound feet will be a poor mother, incapable of giving a good education to her children, passing only the conventional commands of her husband and mother-in-law on to them. Such a woman cannot be creative herself, nor can she give to her children that valid assistance so essential for the development of a high potential for creativity.

---

[3] As noted by Wang Liu: "The tremendous emphasis upon conformity also helped to produce a type of personality more introspective and circumspect, and less energetic and active than what the Confucian theories originally visualized" (1959, p. 94).

Baden-Powell, the founder of the Scout Movement, never forgot the importance of maternal assistance:

> Undoubtedly the mother's influence gives as a rule the first impetus to character. A mother cannot give that which she does not possess herself. Therefore it is all-important that the mothers of our country should possess character of a high quality in order to inculcate it in their children (-/2001, p. 28)

And how much high quality character can a woman with bound feet have?

5. Another Extinguisher of Creativity: Castration for Punishment and Eunuchism

Introduction

Castration of the male is referred to in Chinese medical history as early as 1100 B.C. and was at first imposed as punishment for crime. Subsequently castration was sought voluntarily as a means of obtaining the lucrative and influential position of eunuchs in the imperial court....There are likewise references to castration in pre-Christian times in other oriental kingdoms such as Egypt, Babylon, and Persia" (O'Donnell, 1967, p. 194).

The punishment of the courtier Hsü Kuang-han

Owing to a mistake or accident he had had the misfortune to suffer the punishment of castration. The incident reveals the starkly cruel nature of the times, for he was subjected to such treatment as a matter of mercy. Hsü Kuang-han had once been attending Wu Ti on an expedition to the shrines and summer retreat of Kan-ch'üan, and on this occasion he had saddled his horse with a fellow courtier's saddle. For this all too understandable error he was brought up on a charge of carelessness and robbery, and it was decided that the crime merited the death penalty. It was only due to the intervention of an imperial edict that such punishment was commuted to that of castration (Loewe, 1974, p. 124).

The punishment of the Grand Historian Ssu-Ma Ch'ien

A single imprudent word was enough to ruin the life of historian Ssu-ma Ch'ien (147-87? B.C) who set the pattern for historical writing in China for the next two thousand years. That imprudent word was "merit" said in front of the imperial council: the merit of general Li Ling who had been accused of being responsible for the loss of a great and bloody battle which so saddened the emperor. Because of his attempt to remind the council of the past loyalty and virtues of Li Ling, Ch'ien was thrown into prison, accused of defaming the Emperor, for which the penalty was death. "Ch'ien begged a reprieve so that he could finish compiling his history. The Emperor, reluctant to lose so expert and energetic an Astrologer Royal, graciously ordered that instead of being executed, Ch'ien should be castrated" (Boorstin, 1983, p. 561).

Given this form of imperial graciousness, who would dare to say the slightest word in opposition to the Emperor? Later, the literati developed a belief "that running the state was the court's business, not theirs; that criticism of the monarch was inconceivable, so inconceivable that even feeling critical must be regarded as a moral failure on the part of the critic to 'identify his likes and dislikes with those of his prince'; and that any sort of political collaboration among members of the bureaucracy was evidence of disloyalty or at best venality" (Nivison, 1959, p. 16).

Eunuchism

Eunuchism, even if less prevalent than footbinding, was equally corrosive because it directly affected the sons of many emperors - future emperors themselves:

> Male infants sired by the emperor were reared in the profound seclusion of the palace, nourished by wet nurses till weaned. Thereafter, the young princes were placed almost exclusively in the hands of eunuchs who cherished the hope of remaining forever near the seat of power. Toward this end, many eunuchs went to exhaustive lengths to win and hold a future emperor's favor. Unscrupulous, power-hungry eunuchs could—and often did—mold a young heir apparent's character to suit their own ambitions. Many a prince became emperor while still a child. By the time he had reached his majority, his

eunuchs had introduced him to enervating promiscuity and other debilitating habits. Once corrupted morally and physically, the new sovereign was a weak-willed tool in the hands of his caretakers—easily convinced that enemies and traitors lurked everywhere in the *Great Without*. In this way, his faith in the legitimate government advisors was destroyed. His only recourse was to depend on his eunuchs for information, counsel, and support. (Anderson, 1990, p. 18)

Fairbank and Goldman (2006) remarked how the Ming emperors (1361-1644) extensively used eunuchs "in administration as well as in military and other matters. Eventually the court would have 70,000 eunuchs" (p. 130). With the help of his eunuchs, Emperor Chu (r. 1368/1382-1398) enforced his despotism:

Eunuchs, despised by the Confucian literati, were given the responsibility for supervising the decorum of ministers in the daily [imperial] audience, and for administering beatings with heavy clubs in the presence of the court on a signal from the emperor to any official who incurred his displeasure. This beating at court, introduced by Chu became a most notorious feature of the Ming government, and in later reigns were a chief means by which eunuchs came to intimidate the officialdom .... After [the first two Ming emperors], the remaining 200 years of Ming rule saw a succession of weak and incompetent rulers who could not realize that ['autocratic potential inherent in their position'], and who delegated their authority by default to their eunuchs with disastrous results, for these assistants practiced the same vicious cruelties with less sense of responsibility and with less administrative ability" (Mote, 1961, pp. 27, 37).

In essence, eunuchism introduced a major note of debasement and cruelty: on the eunuchs themselves, and on society at large.

6. The Ultimate Killer of Creativity: The Emperor

Truth is whatever the Emperor says

Emperor Yung-cheng (r. 1723-35) of the Ch'ing dynasty demanded that his officials trust him utterly. This trust, as demanded in his edict of 1724, was to exclude their placing any trust in themselves or in one another. Not only were they to trust his good faith and his ability to distinguish between sincere and insincere counsel; they were to accept his 'preferences' as virtually making the distinction between right and wrong, good and bad:

> Worthy men are the men of whom We approve, and you ought to approve of them; unworthy men are the men We dislike, and you ought therefore to dislike them.... A man's greatest duties are his duty to his prince and his duty to his parents.... In sum, only if each man takes his prince's likes and dislikes as his own will everyone be able to reform his evil ways and turn to good. For prince and minister to be of one mind means good fortune for the state. (Nivison, 1959, p. 228)

> In the Ch'ing [dynasty, 1644-1912], by the eighteenth century, Chinese despotism had become as perfect as human things become; not only was the emperor's command of political power unqualified, but his moral authority, even his intellectual authority, was paramount, and the literati now accepted this situation as natural and right. (ib., p. 23)

The consequence was that creativity diminished in direct proportion to the extent of the imperial power:

> Innovators and purveyors of foreign ideas were regarded as troublemakers and were suppressed.... The Ming [1368-1644] and Quing [1644-1911] emperors were more absolute and autocratic than their predecessors. Before them, coups d'état and regicides occurred frequently, thus introducing an element of 'competition' into the Chinese political market. Rigid etiquette and complete obedience and conformism became the hallmark of the Chinese government under the Ming emperors. (Mokyr, 1990, pp. 231, 237)

Secret-police

There are still other reasons for speaking of a totalitarian state. In the first place, there was a secret-police atmosphere of mutual suspicion, in which everyone kept watch on everyone else. Then there was the arbitrary character of justice. In the eyes of the authorities, every accused person was assumed to be guilty. Terror was instilled by the principle of collective responsibility, making every subject shake in his shoes, and the scholar-officials most of all, for, although they ruled the state, they were also its servants. (Balazs, 1964, p. 17)

"Most vicious of Chu's [Yüan-chang (1723-1735)] new institutions was the *Chin-i-wei*, a secret police unit which had the power to arrest any person at any time, incarcerate him for any length of time, and inflict any manner of torture on him in order to prepare a case against him" (Mote, 1961, p. 28). But even earlier, "A survey of the Han bureaucracy [206 BC-AD 220] reveals that out of some 1300 officials on whom we have relevant information more than a third died a violent death outside the battlefield, the great majority at the hands of the state or by suicide induced by actual or expected charges against them" (Wittfogel, 1957, p. 357).

Cruelty

[During the reign of Emperor Chu], the number put to death in the Hu Wei-yung case in 1380 is said to have been in excess of 30,000, and in the LanYü case ten years later more than 15,000. These great blood-letting conveniently got rid of all manner of old associates of the emperor, and other possibly ambitious men, and they terrorized the whole of officialdom.... Often it was the cruelty of the execution that accomplished the great terrorization. Many new means of slowly and painfully separating the body from the spirit were made regular punishment; they included beating the victim with sand bags without breaking his skin until his whole body was a balloon of jelly, including a lingering and painful death; alternate scalding with boiling water and scrubbing with wire brushes; and ling-ch'ih, which meant slowly slicing a man to pieces with a prescribed 3,357 strokes of the knife, with a pause after each ten strokes to permit him to recover his feelings.... In front of all local government offices was a 'skinning place' where the whole skin was peeled from the body of the corrupt official, and filled with straw to make an effigy which was then hung there to warn his successor and associates. (Mote, 1961, p. 28)

The system was additionally vicious because not only was the individual sliced to pieces, but all his close male relatives aged sixteen or over were summarily executed by beheading or strangulation, and all the women and minor males in the family were enslaved[4]. In such conditions, who would dare to be a hero for the common good?

7. The Mandarins: the Emperor's Long Hands

A final totalitarian characteristic was the state's tendency to clamp down immediately on any form of private enterprise (and this in the long run kills not only initiative but even the slightest attempts at innovation), or, if it did not succeed in putting a stop to it in time, to take over and nationalize it.... To avoid getting into trouble was the Chinese bureaucrat's main concern, and he always managed to saddle his responsibilities on to some subordinate who could serve as a scapegoat.... The virtues preached by Confucianism were exactly suited to the new hierarchical state: respect, humility, docility, obedience, submission, and subordination to elders and betters....

The "protection" of the mandarinate was a heavy burden, but there was no social group strong enough to protect [the individual] against the mandarinate. *This is the exact opposite of what happened in Europe. There, the serf was able to take refuge in free towns under the protection of the autonomous bourgeoisie. This is where the heart of the matter lies: Chinese towns, far from being the bulwark of freedom, were the seats of the mandarinate, the centers of state administration....*The scholar-officials' state was so strong that the merchant class never dared to fight it openly in order to extract from it liberties, laws, and autonomy for themselves. (Balazs, 1964, pp. 18-23; my italics)

8. The Unity of Power of the Scripts

Further detrimental to creativity, was that
the Chinese examination system also perpetuated a high culture common to all the gentry.... The questions themselves were based upon Confucian classics which the candidates were all expected to memorize in advance. Thus, however different their regional or social backgrounds, all scholar-officials wrote a universally understood classical Chinese and had educated

---

[4] See Spence's 2001 discussion of emperors Yongzheng and Qianlong (r. 1723-1796), and Mirsky, 2001, pp. 39-40).

themselves with an identical set of Confucian texts.... Unfortunately, the examination system placed a premium upon the rote learning of works which the government had decided were orthodox. Critics of the Chinese system argued that it stultified creative thought and rewarded drones rather than original intellects" (Wakeman, 1975, p. 23).

Thus, all educated people thought alike and were unable to interact critically with each other or with the system.

9. The Contrast Between Japan and China

Lawrence Harrison in *Who Prospers? How Cultural Values Shape Economic and Political Success* of 1992, asked "Why did Japan drive itself to modernity, and equality with the West, while Ch'ing China [1644-1912] gradually disintegrated?" (p. 132). My answer is that the Japanese ethnopsychology was not *insular* but *strict-ritter*[5] under the impact of the partial unity/partial division of power which ruled Japan for so long: the power of the emperor in Kyoto, of the shogun in Edo, and of the roughly 300 daimyo (feudal lords) and their samurai in the provinces (a situation well described in the famous play *Chûshingura* on the heroism, inconceivable in China, of the 47 *ronin* [masterless samurai] of Lord Asano.

The scenario of the play describes that every year two daimyo had to make all out efforts to honor the emperor, thereby keeping alive the script which stressed the importance of the emperor in Japanese affairs, even if without actual power in day-to-day operations, a situation which spared the emperor from making errors and unpopular decisions. Thus when Japan suffered from the arrival of foreigners in the 1850's (e.g., the warships of Commodore Perry in 1853) it was the shogunate who bore the responsibility while the emperor in Kyoto could act as the savior, and return to actual power in 1868.

Throughout, even to the end (with the ritual suicide of the 47 ronin in Edo/Tokyo), *Chushingura* is a story of the impact of the partial division of power—between emperor, shogun, daimyo, samurai,

---

[5] *Ritter* (knight/warrior) is the personality of those raised under the local power of a prince, who takes direct supervision over his people, demanding, through "stick and carrot", fidelity, discipline, hard work, courage, and focused initiative. *Strict-ritter* are those raised under the strict direction of a Japanese daimyo.

ronin—in strong contrast to the high imperial unity of power narrated in *The Dream of the Red Chamber*, the greatest masterpiece of traditional Chinese fiction, written at about the same time as *Chushingura*. The stark difference between these two forms of power is the answer to both the Needham and Harrison questions.

2

Solving the Enigma of the Constant Low Creativity in Imperial Byzantium

1. Comparing and contrasting the Christian East with the Christian West

Why was the Byzantine civilization (330-1453 AD) always so low in creativity?

For McNeill (1963) "it was the Greco-Roman and Judeo-Christian inheritance, which however attenuated during the Dark Ages, that provided the fundamental frame for the elaboration of high medieval and modern [Western] European civilization" (p. 539). The Byzantines had this same "Greco-Roman and Judeo-Christian inheritance;" however this did not help them to be creative, as it did in the West.

Some of the greatest gifts that Byzantium gave to the West were a mastery of the Greek language, and a trove—and love—of classical texts[6]; therefore, on this, the Byzantines werefar better placed to be creative.

---

[6] "We have no difficulty recognizing that we owe Byzantium for the transmission of the Greek literary and philosophical traditions; had it not been for the preservation of the Greek learning and literature in the Eastern Empire, our own fifteenth-century would have taken a profound different turn. But it is often forgotten that how we approach Greek culture is also in very large part a result of what Western scholars learned from their Byzantine teachers. Similarly, we remember that the great Byzantine theologians made important contributions.... These are only two of the ways that Byzantium has influenced Western civilization directly. It has influenced it indirectly in many more ways, as literary inspiration, as a dream, as a model, etc." (White, 1966, p. ix).

Could it be that the Byzantine Greco-Roman and Judeo-Christian inheritance was too strong, casting too large a shadow? Or, could it be that the low creativity of Byzantium was due to the heavy weight of the combined power of its emperors over both, the state and religion?

2. Low creativity

H. W. Haussig thus summarized the situation in his *A History of the Byzantine Civilization*: "The Byzantines preserved the cultural heritage of ancient Greece but scarcely developed it further" (1971, p. 381).

In Literature and Science

Literature and science are the areas that cause lovers of the Byzantine Civilization to develop excuses, as did Cyril Mango in his *Byzantium: The Imperial Centuries*: "It would be unfair to judge Byzantine literature by the criterion of the aesthetic pleasures it affords to the modern reader.... We appreciate originality, while they prized the cliché; we are impatient of rhetoric, while they were passionately fond of it; we value concision, while they were naturally inclined to elaboration and verbiage" (1980, p. 234).

Others avoided the excuses: "Poetry disappeared, and what passed for it was no more than rhetorical versification, at best ornate and insipid, at worst a detestable jargon. All originality, all freshness, all emotion was stifled" (Jenkins, 1966, p. 385). Similarly, Marshall and Mavrogordato wrote: "Byzantine literature as a whole is not a great literature; few would study it for pleasure unless they were already interested in the culture of the East Roman Empire" (1949, p. 221).

Combining description with explanation, Robert Byron said, in *The Byzantine Achievement*, that "While in literature, save for such scattered exceptions as the hunting epic of Digenis Akritas, the creative powers of the Byzantine were negatived by an excessive appreciation of the past; while in thought, the access to both Hellenic philosophy and Aramean theology, a combination unknown to contemporary Europe, seemed for the most part so amply sufficient as to render superfluous any addition to the beliefs of successive last generations; and while in science the wisdom of the ancient world was conserved and utilized for everyday purposes, rather than increased; in art and architecture, the Byzantines, for those who measure the value of human activity in terms of the divine quest, took strides of incalculable importance, not only in the light of their actual productions, but in their relationship to the whole cultural advance of Europe" (1929, p. 62).

Why was there such an excessive appreciation of the past? Why were there so few efforts to add to philosophy and science? The only way to avoid antagonizing the emperor and his retinue was not to say anything new, not only anything that could be perceived as criticism, but anything unknown to the great man which could force him to admit that others had power, even if only intellectual power. The only way to survive and be creative was to stay firmly "in art and architecture; in forms of religious piety, the liturgy, and ecclesiastical literature; in aspects of philology" (Geanakoplos, 1976, p. 93); or, referring to Robert Byron, to limit one's activity to the "divine quest."

There remained one rhetorical and literary field in which one could be creative, with no limitations: *imperial panegyrics*. "The orator was to recall the emperor's place of origin, his birth, his parents, his education and physical appearance, his deeds in peace and war; he was to portray him as a shining example of the virtues, especially wisdom, courage, justice, and moderation. He should stress his philanthropy and piety. Within this framework, of course, a great many variations were possible" (Dennis, 1997, p. 133).

Not surprisingly, "the modern reader, perhaps, is most struck by the extreme, almost sickening, flattery in these orations, which reminds one of the personality cult accorded to certain dictators in this century.... One wonders how the person so honored could sit and listen without feeling some embarrassment " (ib., p. 134). However, the emperors seldom felt embarrassment, and most often liked these orations, inviting the best speakers back to give yet another speech. Not only the emperor, but also many others in the Empire "firmly believed that, whatever they might think about the individual, the position of the emperor was sacred and worthy of all praise" (ib., p.134). In such *insular* societies, it is difficult to determine later whether the *insularity* is pushed downward from the supremo to the subjects or upward from them to the supremo: they are all prisoners of *insular* scripts, and any change can only come from the exterior.

In the Arts and Architecture

In the arts the lovers of Byzantium are also on the defensive:

> In the first place, Byzantine art, like Byzantine literature, was undeniably very conservative. Since it evolved at a slow pace, the dating of its oeuvre is seldom an easy matter, especially in view of the fact that the great majority of objects and buildings bear no dates. Secondly, Byzantine art was anonymous and impersonal. In the art of western Europe, at any rate since the late Middle Ages, individual personalities attract much of our attention, so that the history of European art does not concern itself merely with the evolution of forms: it is also the story of persons who lived known lives, who introduced innovations, who expressed their opinion on art, who exerted an influence on other known artists. Nothing of the kind applied to Byzantine art. (Mango, 1980, p. 256-7)

Michael Grant also conceded the poverty of literary creativity: "Byzantine literature as a whole is not great literature; although there were a good many poets, notably in Egypt.... So the literature of the period is mostly, as literature, second rate and unoriginal: the educated public of both empires [East and West in the 5th century AD], who were quite numerous, expressed themselves through architecture and, to some extent, visual art, rather than through writings" (1998, p. 77).

But how many educated persons could design new buildings, mosaics, and interior decoration, and thereby express themselves creatively? How many could be creative in the contemplation of somebody else's architectural works? And, how many new ideas, feelings, problems can be expressed and discussed through architecture? Can creativity in architecture be a substitute for creativity in literature? No: lack of creativity in literature is the clearest indicator of a severe case of *insular ethnopsychology*.

Even in architecture, the Byzantines were not original. In discussing the plan of the famous church of St. Sophia in Constantinople, completed in 537, Charles Diehl wrote: "There was doubtless nothing new in such a plan. St. Sophia is related to the type of building, familiar in Asia Minor since the fifth century, known as the domed basilica.

But in virtue of its great size, harmony of lines, boldness of conception, and constructive skill, it appears none the less a true creation" (1949, p. 167). To Emperor Justinian, the basilica was the fulfillment of his dream, and on the day of its inauguration he is reported to have exclaimed, in a transport of enthusiasm: "Thanks be to God who has found me worthy to complete so great a work and to surpass even thee, O Solomon!" (Rice, 1962, p. 76). St. Sophia, therefore, seems to share in the main characteristic of every major architectural work fostered by the unity of power: it is huge—like the Pyramids and the Colosseum—and it exceeds what had been previously constructed.

3. Byzantine Unity of Power, and not Western Division of Power

The Byzantine civilization is different from most other civilizations as it was ruled under the unity of power since its inception. Byzantium started when Emperor Constantine converted to Christianity, combining the power of the state with that of religion. In the words of Jenkins (1966), during the reign of Constantine the Great (324-37):

> The religion of Christ was grafted, with startling ingenuity but not everywhere with absolute harmony, on the existing imperial idea.... The old dogma of the unity of the world beneath the elect of Jupiter, ... was, for practical purpose, modified by the simple substitution of Jesus for Jove. The younger, more mystical Divinity replaced the older and more effete, with an increase in imperial authority and prestige.... Anyone who disagreed ... was God's enemy as well as Rome's.[7] Anyone who refused to submit to the Roman scepter was automatically a rebel, a disturber of God's Peace, in short, a warmonger, to be dealt with righteously as God has dealt with Lucifer-Satan" (Jenkins, 1966, p. 5).

That "grafting of the religion of Christ" went smoothly because it did not imply changes of the power structure: "Since the political authority had descended in a virtually unbroken line from the time of the Caesars, the Eastern Church had developed within the protective

---

[7] The Byzantines referred to themselves as Romans, except late in their history when they took up the old name of Hellenes.

custody of the state, and it accepted the role played by the emperor in church affairs very early" (White, 1966, p. xiii).

>Few rulers in the world have been more powerful than the Emperor of Byzantium. Few states, even in the Middle Ages, have had a more absolute conception of monarchical authority....'Who should be capable of solving the riddles of the law and revealing them to men,' says Justinian, 'if not he who alone has the right to make the law?' By definition, the imperial function conferred upon him who assumed it absolute power and infallible authority" (Diehl, 1957, pp. 28-9).

>[The emperor] was the ultimate authority in the Empire. He could appoint and dismiss all ministers at his will; he had complete financial control; legislation was in his hands alone; he was commander-in-chief of all Imperial forces. He was, moreover, head of the Church, High Priest of the Empire. (Runciman, 1956, p. 51).

>The emperor was, of course, emperor 'by the Grace of God.' More than this, God's grace made him 'holy,' 'divine'; the 'sun on earth.' He was 'equal to the Apostles,' the 'God-resembling Emperor,' and 'a god on earth.' These were not merely high-flown ceremonial phrases; they reflected the very real Byzantine belief that it was possible for God to choose as his instrument a man whose powers then became divine powers.... The Byzantine emperor *was* a Christ-figure; he was not merely the vicar or viceregent of Christ, ruling in his name, but the true imitation or *mimesis* of Christ—a living image. (Miller, 1966, p. 34-6).

It followed that "The powers of the Orthodox Christian Church, as an influence on the workings of the state, were limited formally to participation in the ceremonies which raised a man to the imperial office. Even in this instance—in the ceremony of coronation—the presence of the patriarch does not seem to have been absolutely necessary.... The patriarch, who was by definition a creature of the emperor, only provided the technical approval of the Christian Church organization. God, not the patriarch, chose and anointed the emperor" (ib., pp. 31-2).

Specifically, the emperor "ruled the Church as he ruled the State, nominating bishops for election, consecrating them, and, if they proved insufficiently amenable to his will, dismissing them. He legislated in religious as in secular matters, summoning ecclesiastical councils, guiding their debates, confirming their canons, and carrying their resolutions into effect; and those who rebelled against the imperial will rebelled against God Himself. He drafted rules for ecclesiastical discipline and did not hesitate to fix dogmas" (Diehl, 1957, p. 33).

In consequence, "The Byzantine rulers never became involved in anything resembling the Investiture Controversy in the medieval Western Empire—in any clash of church and state—because the emperor had been from the first much more than merely a political figure" (Miller, 1966, p. 35). Here, the unity of power is as strong as that of the later pharaohs, and with the same negative impact on creativity. Here, the "never anything resembling the Investiture Controversy" points to the most vital difference between Eastern and Western Christendom, between the West and other civilizations.

3

Solving the Enigma of the Decline of Creativity in the Arab World

1. Overview

The Four Ages of Creativity of the Arab World
1. Early Period to A.D. 750
2. Age of Translation from about 750 to about 900
3. The Golden Age from about 900 to about 1100
4. Age of Decline from about 1100[8]

The Four Ages of Conversion to Islam
1. Up to A.D. 750, few had converted [9]
2. By the 11th century many had converted, but they were not the majority
3. In the 12th century, there were no more Christians in the Maghrib, still many in Egypt
4. In the 15th century, practically everybody was Islamized [10]

Between the years 630 and 740 the Arab armies rapidly created a huge empire linked by the same language and religion,

---

[8] Meyerhof (1931, p. 31).
[9] "At the end of the Omayadage [750 A.D.] the majority of the population of Syria, Egypt and Iraq was still Christian" (Saunders, 1965, p. 81).
[10] "By the 15th century the flood of Arabic Islam had covered the whole region" (Hourani, 1991, p. 96).

with ease of travel and commerce among its various parts. An explosion of creativity followed in most fields (science, technology, the arts), especially in the Middle East, North Africa, and in Spain. This came from the release of local energies under the tolerant *Pax Islamica* replacing more totalitarian foreign rules (e.g., those of Byzantine, and the Visigoths). At the same time it was impossible for the invading Arab armies to rapidly impose their religion and culture on the conquered people and to exert a detailed control over them which meant a practical division of power in many fields. This, in turn, was highly conducive to cross-fertilization and to creativity. "The eighth to the twelfth century AD was the period of Islamic glory. It was a period in which the Muslims developed a thirst for learning—a craving, the like of which history had never known before....It was in the field of natural sciences, in particular [astronomy, mathematics, physics, geography, biology, medicine, and chemistry] that they made outstanding advances and achieved the greatest triumphs" (Qadir, 1988, p.104). "There can be no doubt that the philosophers and scientists, geographers, natural historians and medical men of Arabian culture contributed materially to the sum of man's knowledge about the natural world. This was part of their bequest to the late medieval West" (Ronan, 1983, p.239).

However, over the centuries, first a religious and then a cultural uniformity developed through the conversion to Islam of ever larger segments of the population. The great majority came under the power of the religious purists who hated the new and saw creativity as a betrayal of long established and all encompassing invariable truths:

[To the Muslim religious purist] history is a series of accidents that in no way affect the nontemporal principles of Islam. He is more interested in knowing and "realizing" these principles than in cultivating originality and change as intrinsic virtues. The symbol of Islamic civilization is not a flowing river, but the cube of the Kaaba, the stability of which symbolizes the permanent and immutable character of Islam. Once the spirit of the Islamic revelation had brought into being, out of the heritage of previous civilizations and through its own genius, the civilization whose manifestations may be called distinctly Islamic, the main interest turned away from change and "adaptation." The arts and sciences came to possess instead a stability and a "crystallization" based on the immutability of the principles from which they had issued forth; it is this stability that is too often mistaken in the West today for stagnation and sterility. (Nasr,1968/1992, p. 21)

2. DP learning from advanced cultures

The biggest single influence which helped to shape it [the rise of the Arabic civilization] was Greek science and philosophy,... Established in an educated society, the invaders grew ashamed of their ignorance, and the Caliphs encouraged learned Christians and Jews to turn these books [the leading works of Greek medicine and methaphisics] into the dominant language of the Empire. This translating went on for some two centuries (800-1000), at the close of which educated Muslims could read the masters of Hellenic thought in Arabic versions of Syriac translations of the Greek originals. (Saunders, 1965, p. 190)

3. Learning to defend themselves in debates with learned Christians

The immediate source of the spark which ignited the fire of intellectual activity and translation of Greek, Syriac, Pahlavi, and Sanskrit texts into Arabic, more than any possible utilitarian motives to benefit from medicine and astrology, was the debates held in Damascus, Basra, Kufa, Baghdad, and other Muslim cities between Muslims and scholars and theologians of other religions. Often these debates were held in the presence of the caliphs or religious authorities, especially the Shiite Imams. In these debates, where open discussion was usually permitted, the Muslims found themselves on the defensive before the weapons of logic and philosophy with which their adversaries were armed. Soon the Muslims realized that in order to defend the tenets of the faith itself they had to arm themselves with the same weapons. The challenge of a theologian like John the Damascene could only be answered with a theology of similar intellectual content. Therefore, the Muslims sought to master the logic and philosophy of their religious opponents, especially those Christians who were thoroughly acquainted with Greek philosophy and logic. This movement not only led to the concerted effort to translate, leading to the founding of such vast institutions as the

"House of Wisdom" (*Bayt al-hikmah*) of Ma'mún in Baghdad whose specific function was translation of works into Arabic, but it was also instrumental in the particular way in which Muslim theology was formulated, as we see in the case of the Christian hypostases and the Islamic Divine Attributes.

The golden age of translation lasted for a period of nearly 150 years, from about 150 (767) to 300 (912). During this period a large number of basic Greek texts in philosophy and the sciences, in the most general sense, were rendered into Arabic, sometimes directly from the Greek, at other times through the intermediary of Syriac. Special attention was paid to the works of Aristotle and his commentators, of which there are more translations in Arabic than in European languages, and also to classical mathematical and astronomical treatises such as those of Euclid, Archimedes, and Ptolemy. Medico-philosophical treatises, especially those of Galen, were also translated extensively as were many works in the occult sciences whose original Greek or Syriac version is lost. In fact Arabic is today a valuable source of knowledge for Greek philosophy and science, especially of the later period, precisely because of the large number of texts translated and preserved as well as the high quality of many of the translations. Altogether from the point of view of quality and quantity alike the transmission of the learning of the ancient world to Muslims through the medium of Arabic is one of the most startling phenomena of cultural history; for not only was it instrumental in bringing into being Muslim sciences and philosophy but it also played indirectly a vital role in the creation of medieval and Renaissance science and philosophy in the West, and even influenced China and India. (Nasr, 1973, p. 640)

4. Extensive learning from foreign commerce

As noted by Bernard Lewis,

During the long period of Arab eclipse three significant changes emerge. The first of these is the transformation of the Islamic Near East from a commercial, monetary economy to one which, despite an extensive and important foreign and transit trade, was internally a quasi-feudal economy, based on subsistence agriculture. (1947/93, p. 174)[11]

If there is a true hero in *The Thousand Nights and One Night* it is a merchant: Sindbad the Sailor or Seaman, travelling widely, and upon his return, narrating his adventures with gusto. These stories include descriptions of other peoples, often told with admiration, which would not be possible in later fundamentalist times:

> While I lived in that isle, I had occasion to hear and see many astonishing things. I will tell you a few of them:
>
> One day, while I was in the presence of King Mihrjan, I was introduced to certain Indians, who willingly answered the questions which I put to them. They informed me that in their country, which is called India, there are a great number of castes, of which the two most important are Kshatriya and Brahman. The first is composed of well-born and equitable men, who are never guilty of sin or oppression; and the second of pure and holy people who never drink wine and yet are friends of joy, of good manners, of horses, of pageantry and beauty. The learned Indians also told me that these castes are divided into seventy-two lesser castes, whose traditions are separate in every way. This astonished me a great deal. (-/1986, 2, pp. 183-84)

It would be hard to be more complimentary, more culturally DP, than in this praise of a non-Muslim world in which equitable men prosper, "who are never guilty of sin or oppression .... pure and holy people who never drink wine and yet are friends of joy, of good manners...". On a smaller scale we are reminded of the encounters between Medieval Italian and Muslim merchants discussed by Sapori:

> But here and there, a sense of business survived in the face of martial spirit, and this was regarded as a sign of irresponsibility by the prejudiced. When they met each other during the truces, Italians and Mohammedans violated the precepts of their respecive religions, a sign of a lack of principles, but also a

---

[11] "The second is the end of the political independence of the sedentary Arab and Arab-speaking people and their replacement by the Turk.... The third change is the shifting of the centre of gravity of the Arab-speaking world from Iraq to Egypt" (ib., p. 174).

proof of vitality. Because of this, the contacts and collisions that put these two peoples in the presence of each other were not as sterile as the consequences of warfare alone would have been. (1948/1970, p. 7)

Not only were these contacts not sterile, rather they were creativogenic in reducing the strength of the common scripts and in suggesting new ways of thinking and doing—valuable new scripts.

It is from Sindbad the Merchant[12], in his explanation to his friends as to why he undertook a second voyage, that we get a perfect description of the curious and enterprising mentality of the creative centuries of Islam:

> I was living a life of unexampled pleasure, when, one day, the old desire entered my head to visit far countries and strange people, to voyage among the isles and curiously regard things hitherto unknown to me; also the trading habit rose in me again. I went to the market and spent a great deal of money on suitable merchandise, which I had solidly packed and taken to the quay. There I soon found a fair new ship, equipped with excellent sails, having every sort of marine mechanism aboard and a stout crew of excellent sailors. I fell in love with this vessel, and caused all my goods to be taken aboard and placed with those of other merchants, who were known to me and with whom I was very pleased to journey. (ib., p. 187)

This interest in "far countries and strange people" and "things hitherto unknown" was shared by the elite of his city of Baghdad:

---

[12] Sindbad the Merchant should be the real name, not the Sailor or Seaman as in most translations, because he was a rich merchant of Baghdad, the son of a rich merchant of that city, the city of Caliph Harun al-Rashid (766-809).

At the end of his sixth voyage Sindbad meets Harun al-Rashid bringing him a letter and precious gifts from the distant King of Sarandid. In turn his seventh voyage begins with the Caliph asking him to return to the King with an answer and many more gifts. We are here reminded that "Diplomatic missions were exchanged between Charlemagne and Harun al-Rashid, in the course of which the Caliph sent, among other gifts, an elephant to the Frankish Emperor, and granted special facilities to Frankish pilgrims visiting the Holy Places in Palestine" (Saunders, 1965, p. 115).

Sindbad's stories (already part of a 9th century version of the *Nights*) are representative of the general curiosity of the Age of Translation of 750-900.

[Upon returning from his second voyage]

Every day important people came to hear me speak of my adventures and to learn how things went in far-off lands; and I rejoiced to entertain and teach them in the way they wished. They would never leave without first congratulating me on my escape from such terrible dangers and expressing a pleasant surprise at all I told them. (ib., p. 194)

But things changed when most important people began to share the same deeply felt creed, and had been convinced by religious purists to avoid an interest in the religion and mores of non-Muslim people who certainly were neither pure nor holy.

Once the important people had curtailed their interest in foreign goods and stories, there was no reason to go abroad and to play the Sindbad; it was safer to stay at home and court those in power who had no reason to oppose the religious majority which demanded the least amount of novelty and information on other people.

5. No longer learning from advanced cultures

For more than four hundred years the most fruitful work in mathematics, astronomy, botany, chemistry, medicine, history and geography, was produced in the world of Islam by Muslims and Christians, Jews and Zoroastrians, pagans and Manichaeans.... Yet this brilliant culture, which shone so brightly in contrast to the darkness of the Latin West and the stagnation of Byzantium, began to fade from the thirteenth century onwards. Arabic philosophy was dead by 1200, Arabic science by 1500. The nations of Western Europe, once sunk in barbarism, caught up and overtook the peoples of Islam. How did this come about? The question has hardly yet received a complete and satisfactory answer, but some tentative suggestions may be offered...

Probably the biggest factor was the strongly religious character of Islam itself and the absence of a vigorous pre-Islamic secular tradition. Behind Christian Europe lay the science and rationalism of classical Greece: Behind Islam lay nothing save the cultural poverty of 'the days of ignorance.' The Muslims did, as we have seen, borrow a good deal from Greece, but in a limited and indirect fashion: the Greek past never *belonged* to them in the sense in which it did to Christendom, and there was never a joyous acceptance or recovery of it as took place in the West at the time of the Renaissance. The spirit of Islam was not rational in the Greek sense of the term, in that God is beyond reason and his ordering of the universe is to be accepted rather than explained. True knowledge is that of God and his Law, and the law embraces all human activity: secular learning for its own sake to be strongly discouraged, and intellectual pursuits are permissible only insofar as they further a deeper piety and understanding of religious truth....

The shift in outlook became noticeable in the Seljuk age. The great Ghazzali [1058-1111] devoted his life to the defence of Koranic truth against what he regarded as the insidious encroachments of unbelief. Islamic dogma was linked with Sufi mysticism. Muslim education was geared to the new orthodoxy by the founding of *madrasas*, where the religious sciences alone received intensive study. The Shari'a came to dominate Muslim life as the Torah had dominated post-exilic Judaism. The door was closed against further borrowings from outside: philosophy was repudiated as a danger to the Faith, because it was alleged to deny a personal God, creation *ex nihilo*, and the resurrection of the body. (Saunders, 1965, pp. 195-97)

That shift in outlook became noticeable when first a religious and then a cultural uniformity developed through the conversion to Islam of ever larger segments of the population, with even changes of name, for instance from Persian to Arab:

One is astonished to see how thoroughly the former became Arabicised in the course of a few generations.... They assumed Arabic names and sought to disguise their foreign extraction by fair means or foul. Many provided themselves with fictitious pedigree, on the strength of which they passed for Arabs. Such a pretense could have deceived nobody if it had not been supported by a complete assimilation in language, manners, and even to some extent in character. (Nicholson, 1907/1993, pp. 280-81)

With the absence of religious opponents there was no longer a reason to spend time studying non-Islamic texts. On the contrary, the demand for Islamic purists accelerated; purists free of old pagan thoughts, like al-Ghazzali who advanced because what he was saying was desired by the majority.

This problem is not new: scholars are open minded and democratic when they belong to a minority; they instead become intolerant and absolutist when they preach to their own strong majority.

Another piece of evidence for pointing the finger at a massive conversion to Islam comes from reading of the miseries suffered by Averroes in Spain (1126-1198), the influential religious philosopher who integrated Islamic tradition and Greek thought:

> Shortly after [1195], Averroes suddenly lost the favor of [caliph] Al-Mansour; all his works that were not strictly on science were ordered to be burned and he was exiled. He was insulted by mobs, and his disciples abandoned him. Various reasons for Averroes' disgrace have been suggested, but the most likely explanation is that the humiliation of Averroes was a move of political expediency on the part of the caliph. The Muwahhid dynasty of which the caliph was a member had originated in an atmosphere of religious fanaticism; and when now and then there was a renewal of strong religious feeling stemming from the people, the caliph would burn the books of the philosophers and temporarily—though regretfully—persecute the philosophers until the people were appeased. Once the danger had passed, the philosophers could secretly be restored to favor. (Zedler, 1961, p. 10)

Grunebaum (1970) presents another indication of the strong conservative power of the religious community, when it had become the majority:

> The gradual exhaustion of scientific productivity in the twelfth and thirteenth centuries is due to nothing else than a change of interests among the Muslim intelligentsia. The conservation of the *umma* [the religious community] had become a primary preoccupation, and the troubles of the time, soon made more oppressive by the assault of the heathen Mongols, required all its strength to maintain the Community intact. En-

ergies had to be concentrated and men had to forgo the luxury of extending those branches of knowledge that were indifferent to religion, and even possibly dangerous. The security of the Community lay in the certainty of the apostolic tradition. Everything new was rejected and feared more than ever before, and consequently any research that gave itself out as original or indeed any activity which distracted from the religious goal of life. In spite of intellectual agitation the period was anti-intellectual, even anti-rational. Gnosis or intuition stood high above the knowledge gained by thinking; tradition, not reason deserved trust; faith blunted the critical will and the critical ability. Religious satisfaction was derived from the fallibility of the human mind; man's weakness was God's glory, humility before God his only honour. (p. 198)

External difficulties certainly played a role, but the changes of ethnopsychology were more important: a diverse, *quasi-visitor* society had transformed itself into a uniform, compact, *insular* community which had lost the capability of appreciating the new. Everybody thought the same, everything new was rejected and feared. It was the end of creativity: "The arts and sciences [as noted by Nasr] came to possess instead a stability and a "crystallization" based on the immutability of the principles from which they had issued forth" (1968/1992, p. 21).

While the orthodoxy of early Islam tolerated the sciences, we may say that from the time of the famous teacher al-Ghazzali (d. 1111) onwards, this tolerance gave place to persecution of these studies "because they lead to loss of belief in the origin of the world and in the creator." Whether or not this attitude was alone sufficient to prevent the rise of great independent thinkers, it was certainly a very important factor in their suppression. The twelfth century marks a standstill. The works of Rhazes, Avicenna, and Jabir are reproduced, summarized, commented on, but outstanding and independent works are becoming rare. (Meyerhof, 1931, pp. 337-38)

Giorgio de Santillana, in his Preface to Nasr's *Science and Civilization in Islam* was more critical of al-Ghazzali than both Meyerhof and Saunders:

The decline of science inside a great culture is in itself a fascinating study and a terrible object lesson. We can find here the key, in the documents that allow us to judge for ourselves, of the showdown between Averroes and al-Ghazzali. Averroes speaks with the clarity and passionate honesty that we would expect of him, for here was the great Greek tradition at bay, whereas al-Ghazzali's famous eloquence, undistinguished intellectually as it is, and to us ethically uninspired, went to building up the whirlwind of intolerance and blind fanaticism which tore down not only science, but the very School system and the glorious *ijtihad*, the Interpretation of the Quran. (1968/1992, p. xii)

The decisive factor in the triumph of the sacred sciences was their alliance with popular religious feeling, manifest in the Sufi movement. This alliance was sealed by the life and writings of one of the greatest and by all odds the most influential theologian of Islam, al-Ghazali (1058-1111).

Under the Abbasids, angry Baghdad mobs and distrustful Islamic jurists had joined forces to defeat the first Moslem effort to construct a rationally argued theology....The net result was to throttle almost all innovation in Moslem science and philosophy. Thus by a curious and fateful coincidence, Moslem thought froze into a fixed mold just at the time when intellectual curiosity was awakening in western Europe—twelfth and thirteenth centuries A.D. (McNeill, 1963, pp. 502-03)

However, it was less "a curious and fateful coincidence," than the inescapable consequence of the vast number of fully converted Muslims who demanded the total priority of the religious commands at the expense of everything else. In the absence of a major form of DP, the people concluded that they were "more interested in knowing and 'realizing' [the nontemporal] principles than in cultivating originality and change as intrinsic virtues."

4

Why Did Venice Have No Great Writers When It Had Great Painters, Architects and Musicians?

1. Introduction

Venice is an extraordinary place, praised across several centuries, by such connoisseurs as Goethe and Ruskin, for its architects, painters, and composers. Everybody returns enchanted. However little of this praise goes to its writers. On this point the silence is nearly complete. Indeed, none of the great Italian writers were Venetians, not Dante, Petrarch, Boccaccio, Machiavelli, Ariosto or Tasso. Even the stars of second and third magnitude of Italy's *golden centuries*, like Guicciardini, Castiglione, Pulci, Boiardo, Vasari, were not Venetian.[13][14][15]

---

[13] Dante (born in 1265), Petrarch (1302), Boccaccio (1313), Machiavelli (1469), were all Florentines; Ariosto (1474) came from Mantua-Ferrara, and Tasso (1544) from Sorrento-Naples; Pulci (1432) and Guicciardini (1483) were again Florentines; Castiglione (1478) from Mantua in Lombardy; Boiardo (1441, from Scandiano-Ferrara; Vasari (1511) from Tuscan Arezzo, 40 miles south-east of Florence.

[14] A partial exception could be Paolo Sarpi (b. 1552) the author of *History of the Council of Trent*, first published in London in 1619.

[15] Later there are writers such as Goldoni (b. 1707), and autobiographers like Casanova (b. 1725), but they already belong to a different world: Goldoni wrote his *Mémoires* in French and dedicated them to King Louis XVI, as did Casanova his *Histoire de ma vie* (History of my life).

Others have identified this dearth. Even the philo-Venetian William McNeill, in his *Venice: the hinge of Europe, 1081-1797*, was forced to admit that "until after 1481, when Venice's imperial power was already entering on a downward path, the city remained a follower, not a pace-setter in matters cultural" (1974, p. 92).

On the other hand, as soon as we focus on painting and architecture, Venice is at the forefront: Giovanni Bellini (1430), Carpaccio (1465), Giorgione (1478), Titian (1490) Palladio (1508), Tintoretto (1518), Veronese (1528), were all Venetian.[16] Later a string of great musical composers emerged: Andrea (1510) and Giovanni (1556) Gabrielli, Vivaldi (1665), Albinoni (1674), Alessandro (1684) and Benedetto (1686) Marcello, Tartini (1692), Galuppi (1706).

This combination of few great thinkers (poets, novelists, essayists, philosophers, historians) and many great painters, sculptors, architects and composers is the result of many centuries of unity of power. In the case of Venice it was the unity of power of its oligarchy and of its Byzantine cultural roots.

2. The strong unity of power of the Venetian oligarchy[17]

- *The doge had the right to appoint the Patriarch of Venice and the Canons of St. Mark* and had, among other titles, that of "Most Serene Prince." (Montanelli&Gervaso, 1967, p. 164).
- The strenuous demands Venetian magistrates made on their citizens' loyalty left scant room for other ties. In particular, *the Venetian clergy were strictly subordinated to secular authorities.* The pope figured more often as a foreign power than as an ecclesiastical superior; and the religious enthusiasm associated with the Dominican and Franciscan friars lapped up against the well-consolidated patterns of Venetian

---

[16] Obviously, great painting, sculpture, and architecture can go along with great writing as proved by the following eminent Florentine (or Tuscan) artists: Giotto (1266), Donatello (1382), Fra Angelico (1395), Ghiberti (1378), Masaccio (1401), Pierodella Francesca (1415), Pollaiuolo (1431), Botticelli (1445), Leonardo da Vinci (1452), Michelangelo (1475).
[17] My italics hereafter.

political and economic behavior without the one much affecting the other, so far at least as public events are concerned. A Venetian Savonarola never arose; religion remained always subject to civic and secular control. *"Veneziani, poi Christiani!* [Venetians first, then Christians!]" accurately sums up the city's relationship to Latin Christendom, insofar as Latinity found its Christian expression in obedience to the pope. (McNeill, 1974, p. 92-3)

[On the other hand, historians] still speak of a lay and thoroughly politicized Venice, of a "cesarismo veneziano" dedicated to protecting the overriding interests of the state against monastic and ecclesiastical interests. The exercise of jurisdiction over ecclesiastics did not derive, in Sarpi's eyes[18], from an abstract principle of political sovereignty, but from a living tradition which was at once political and religious:"The ground whereby the Republic judges ecclesiastics lies in the fact that it received this power from God at its birth, and that it has exercised it continuously and without interruption whenever it seemed to be to the advantage of the common good, and in the records that survive we see that at all times all kinds of ecclesiastics have been subject to the magistrates on account of any crimes it seemed proper to charge them with. And if popes have passed laws subsequently, the city has not renounced the power given it by God..." (Prodi, 1973, pp. 409-11).

Fascinating! Sarpi's argument is nearly identical to that used by Emperor Henry IV against Pope Gregory VII, during the *Investiture Controversy*, which said, in essence, that the (German) king and emperor had always been *rex et sacerdos* by the pious ordination of God, and that kings and emperors had always designated and invested bishops. Gregory's opposite answer was equally clear: "The Lord has not said 'I am Tradition,' but 'I am the Truth'" (quoted by Tellenbach, 1936/1991, p. 164).

Even stronger than the position of Emperor Henry IV, is the one taken by Venice as "direct religious follower of Byzantium":

Sarpi's frequent references to the model of the imperial church of Constantine, Theodosius and Justinian are well

---

[18] Paolo Sarpi (1552-1623) patriot, scholar, and state theologian during Venice's struggle with Pope Paul V.

known.... Venice still regarded itself as the true heir of the [Roman/Byzantine] imperial Church: the doge, *princeps in republica* and *princeps in ecclesia*. (Prodi, 1973, p. 413)

There is indeed, no stronger unity of power than that which combines in one person or hierarchy the command of the state and of the church! At this point we can refer to what the eminent Belgian historian Henri Pirenne said on the Venetian Byzantine roots:

At the date the city [Venice] was founded, all Italy still belonged to the Byzantine Empire. Thanks to her insular situation, the conquerors who successively overran the peninsula—first the Lombards, then Charlemagne, and finally, still later, the German emperors—were not successful in their attempts to gain possession. She remained, therefore, under the sovereignty of Constantinople, thus forming at the upper end of the Adriatic and at the foot of the Alps an isolated outpost of the Byzantine civilization. While Western Europe was detaching herself from the east, she continued to be part of it. And this circumstance is of capital importance. The consequence was that Venice did not cease to gravitate in the orbit of Constantinople. Across the waters, she was subject to the attraction of that great city and herself grew great under its influence. (1925/1969, p. 83-84)

The consequence, also, was that Venice's literary output was not much higher than that of Byzantium. As in Byzantium, but not elsewhere in Christendom: "Art was at the service of the state in Venice, with an intensity not paralleled elsewhere in Italy.... In order to celebrate themselves, influential men had to glorify the state by showing themselves in service of it" (Wills, 2001, p. 21).

3. Down-to-earth *fox*[19] ideas

The most general element in the political ideal to which Venetian writers exposed their audience was a ubiquitous secularism.... expressed rather in an antipathy to speculative systems that impose an

---

[19] One seems to read from Isahia Berlin's definition of the *fox thinkers* "who pursue many ends... moving on many levels, seizing upon the essence of a variety of experiences and objects for what they are in themselves, without, consciously or unconsciously, seeking to fit them into, or exclude them from, any one unchanging, all embracing, unitary inner vision" (1953/1967, pp. 1-2).

artificial coherence on all values and experience and thereby claim a right to supervise, among other matters, the political order. They were enemies not of religion but of metaphysics, and of the notion that the conduct of human affairs should be determined by some comprehensive vision of the nature of things....The Venetian approach to human affairs was earthbound and empirical. Its refusal to force that data of human experience into large systems was notably exhibited *in the preference of Venetian writers for exposition through dialogues in which various points of view may find expression without explicit resolution.* (Bouwsma, 1990, p. 267, my italics)

4. The secret police

> [The members of the all-powerful Council of Ten] could not leave Venice except on emergencies, and three times a week they held audience for spies and informers. In other words, they were a real secret police, an early version of the NKVD. (Montanelli & Gervaso, 1967, p. 166)

> There was no appeal against their decision. The only constitutional hold on them was the fact that they were elected by the Great Council, annually and then every six months, and for a limited period which started at ten days and then by stages became permanent. Really it created a police state; and some people date Venice's decline from this point. It was started [in 1325] to stamp out the last traces of a conspiracy in 1310. Everyone outside the nobility now knew that their role was to watch and listen. And it says volumes for the genius of the noble class that the ordinary people and the middle class were happy to do this for another half millennium....
>
> The dark Venice that has frightened historians ever since it came into being in the fourteenth century; it was government as conceived by the military, a régime supported by spies and secret murders. The three "inquisitors of state", as they came to be called, grew out of the Ten, as its secret committee.... The Three could punish an offender secretly or publicly as they thought expedient for the state. The stifling *piombi* (cells under the prison roof) and the sodden *pozzi* (at canal level) were at their service. They could draw any amount of money from the treasury of

the Ten without explanation. Even the identity of the Inquisitors was not revealed....

The fact was that the governing families could never rely on themselves to keep order. That was why they elected despots, and needed the despotism while hating and fearing it. That was the reason first of all for the Ten and then for the brisker version of the Ten in the Three.... But no inflexible police state could have lasted even the five hundred years Venice did last after the Closing of the Council, let alone a thousand. Her secret was that her nobles shared not only the fruits of despotism but the discipline as well. (Rowdon, 1970, pp. 16-19)

The Council of Ten took the initiative in internal police. It was on the look-out to suppress not only any possibility of armed insurrection. but of nobles acting as if above the law, and any attempt to organize a faction or party even if merely by soliciting and swapping votes. They permitted no organized opposition...Both the Inquisitors and Council of Ten had strict rules of procedure to follow in passing judgment and inflicting punishment; but their proceedings were secret. The accused had no chance to face accusers, to hire lawyers,or to know fully the case against him. Judgments could not be appealed, and they were sometimes executed with unseemly speed. (Lane, 1973, pp. 117, 404)

5. The cause

I have no doubt that the major cause of Venice's lack of great writers was the first of the three discussed above, that of the Unity of Power of state and church, of the Venetian oligarchy. A major Division of Power, as existed in Florence, would have limited the power of the aristocrats and greatly reduced the power of the police. The DP provides conflicting ideas and data, which can then be compared, accepted, refused, or overcome. Only the Division of Power provides the valid elements for a network of dialectical creativity. The Unity of Power, instead, provides one single truth, the one that the *supremo*-likes.

The initial sparks of creativity come from the clash of personal scripts with those of society in a major *war of the scripts*. However, if the scripts of society are so powerful, accepted by all, never questioned, never debated, then the individual *war of the scripts*, if any, will be limited to down-to-earth matters (e,g., some technical creativity), or, in the higher spheres of creativity, to the visual and auditory domains (painting, sculpture, architecture, music). As seen above: "Art was at the service of the state in Venice, with an intensity not paralleled elsewhere in Italy" (Wills, 2001, p. 21).

6. The Decline

> [Today Florence and Venice] seem to stand in contrast to each other. Florence has become a bustling and vital modern city. Whilst it may no longer nurture Michelangelos and Botticellis, there are native Florentine painters of international renown. Its ancient craft of leatherwork plays a distinctive role in contemporary fashion, and Florentines have effectively revived the old skills with stuffs and dyes and organized their distribution on a scale which dwarfs the network of the once ubiquitous Medici banks.
>
> Venice instead is apparently a city belonging only to her past, an empty shell of former glories. Its native population diminishes constantly, deserting the island for the industrial wasteland that threatens to destroy what is left of millennial grandeur. Its last remaining industry makes baubles for the tourists who come in droves to stay on a statistical average of about eighteen hours, to mill about and to gawk at the remaining relics of the *Serenissima's* magnificence. (Lauritzen, 1978, p. 11)

The death of Venice had been predicted, pronounced, and lamented for two hundred years, ever since 1797, when Napoleon brought the once-mighty Venetian Republic to its knees. At the height of its glory, Venice had been the world's supreme maritime power. Its reach had extended from the Alps to Constantinople, and its wealth had been unequaled. The architectural variety of her palaces—Byzantine, Gothic, Renaissance, baroque, neoclassical—chronicled an evolving aesthetic shaped by a millennium of conquests and their accumulated spoils.

But by the eighteenth century, Venice had given itself over to hedonism and dissipation—masked balls, gaming tables, prostitution, and corruption. The ruling class abandoned its responsibilities, and the state became enfeebled, powerless to resist Napoleon's approaching army. The Great Council of the Venetian Republic voted itself out of existence on May 12, 1797, and the last in the line of 120 doges resigned. From that day forward, there had been no doges in the Doge's Palace, no Council of Ten in the Great Council Chamber, no shipbuilders turning out warships in the Arsenal, no prisoners shuffling across the Bridge of Sighs on the way to the dungeons....Venice emerged from its defeat an impoverished provincial village, unable to do much more than settle into a languid and picturesque decline. It is this Venice that we have come to know—not the triumphant and arrogant conqueror but the humbled and crumbling ruin....

This much I know: The population of Venice had been declining steadily for the past forty-five years—from 174,000 in 1951 to 90,000 at the time of the Fenice fire [of January 26, 1996]. The rising cost of living and the scarcity of jobs had caused a migration to the mainland. (Berendt, 2005, pp. 43-45)

By the middle of the seventeenth century, if not before, the most active centers of creativity in Europe had moved north of the Alps....It did not take the peoples of eastern Europe long to notice what had happened. Peter the Great went to Holland (1697) to see how ships were built and never thought of visiting the Venetian Arsenal, once so famous; and leading Greek intellectuals soon discovered that there were more interesting new ideas to be gleaned in Amsterdam, Paris, and London than in [Venetian] Padua. (McNeill, 1974, p. 217)

Underlying Venetian light-heartedness was the absence in all except a small minority of any serious purpose arising from political involvement. Even the handful of nobles who were thoroughly committed, who ruled the state and made that their lives, lacked stamina and courage. (Lane, 1973, p. 434).

The quality of the doges went down. Good men no longer relished the job, always an empty one, and in any case the electors usually opposed good men. Money had always, since at least the fourteenth century, changed hands in a ducal election. But now money was the only influence. Venice was being sucked dry to keep its aristocracy at the gambling tables....The

Arsenal was a thorough mess, though it continued to have the full complement of men, and cost if anything more to run than in the previous century. Its guild-laws were disregarded. Most of the workmen only turned up for pay-day, and there was no check on the number of their attendances. Some of them took other jobs, while getting full pay. They used the wood meant for ship-building to warm their homes: a government inspector of 1784 said that for some years about seventy thousand faggots had disappeared annually in this way. The apprentices (sons of workmen, by guild law) paid for their certificates of entry instead of studying for them: that is, they paid for their right to get a life-long salary for doing nothing. When Napoleon cleared out the Arsenal he found most of the ships badly fitted, and some not even sea-worthy. (Rowdon, pp. 129-130)

The decline of Venice in the XVIIIth century is due to important conflicts and tensions, and to a difficult cultural circulation ... The books of the Enlightenment were widely read: *nevertheless they did not give origin to thoughts of reform which could seriously tackle the problems of the Republic.* (Ferroni, 1991b, p. 407)

Dogmatic rigidity that had been so energetically imposed on Italian minds by the true believers of the Catholic Reformation also hampered creativity, especially in intellectual and literary fields. This, in turn, was sustained by organizational rigidities that shored up things as they were at the cost of making adjustment to changing circumstances more and more difficult as time went on....Most of all, perhaps, the enormous resources assigned to the support of religious institutions of all kinds sustained and reinforced routine and repetition as the surest way to heaven.... Cultural creativity concentrated therefore on the side of sin: for secular music, theatrical performances, gambling, and other forms of stylish depravity—the fields in which Italy in general and Venice in particular continued to excel the rest of Europe until almost the end of the eighteenth century—all carried with them at least a whiff of brimstone, curable, of course, by a timely resort to the confessional.... *Thus there were strong psychological forces supporting the conservatism of thought and action which dominated Venice from the middle years of the seventeenth century until the final extinction of the Republic in 1797.* (McNeill, 1974, pp. 218-19)

5

The Nile Made the Pharaonic UP Polytheism — the Sea the Greek DP Polytheism

I. Early Egypt

1. Geography

> The Nile made Egypt, and the valley of the Nile was Egypt. Only that part of the country susceptible to flooding could provide a livelihood for the population.... In a sense Egypt was an island, cut off from other habitable lands—to the north by the sea and in all other directions by deserts. Being thus isolated it was both protected from invasion and insulated from external influences. This isolation contributed in no small degree toward the conservative, inward-looking character of life in Egypt. (James, 1978, p. 460)

> Deserts gave the land of Egypt clear-cut and easily defensible boundaries; while the Nile provided it with a natural backbone and nervous system.... The early integration of the land into a single state depended directly upon the easy navigability of the Nile. The flow of the river carried boats northward; and by a lucky chance, the winds of Egypt blow dominantly from the north, so that movement upstream proceeded quite easily with the help of sails. By controlling shipping, the king automatically and easily regulated all major movements of goods and people, and therewith possessed the means for effective rule over Egypt. (McNeill, 1963, pp. 69, 71)

2. The First Stage of UP polytheism: Annexation of the deities of the conquered tribes by the *Supremo*

Prior to the Unification there was a multitude of cults unconnected and entirely localized, each being the particular worship of the god of the tribe. The evolution of these cults was part of the political development of Egypt, for as the tribal areas became welded into principalities and finally into the two separate kingdoms of the North and South, so a mythology was created which united the tribal deities. The god of the conquered tribe was not suppressed but was annexed by the conqueror, who supplanted his defeated predecessor as a son of the deity. These tribal gods became the 'nome' gods of later times and their prerogatives were maintained by the kind, who claimed their special protection, just as in prehistoric times had some long-forgotten chieftain. (Emery, 1961, p. 119)

3. The Second Stage of UP polytheism: Pharaoh, becomes a God

The land of Egypt was not merely governed on behalf of the gods as were, for example, the Sumerian city-states. Egypt was governed by a god and therein lies the fundamental difference between Egyptian concepts of government and those of contemporary peoples. (Ward, 1965, p. 150)

Pharaoh was not mortal but a god. This was the fundamental concept of Egyptian kingship, that Pharaoh was of divine essence, a god incarnate.... In Egypt the community had freed itself from fear and uncertainty by considering its ruler a god. It sacrificed all liberty for the sake of a never changing integration of society and nature....The king of the entire land was not the most successful of a number of chieftains but a ruler without peers. The conquest completed, it became possible to view the unification of Egypt, not as an ephemeral outcome of conflicting ambitions, but as the revelation of a predestined order. And thus kingship was, in fact, regarded throughout Egyptian history.... Pharaoh's predicate "god" found its correlate in his absolute power over the land of Egypt and its inhabitants. Private property appears early as a result of royal donations. But basically it is no more than an exceptional transference of rights.... Even justice is embodied in the god who rules the state; he respects the tradition and the privileges of classes and regions in so far as he approves their fairness; but in principle there is no autonomous justice or law outside that of the Crown. (Frankfort, 1948, pp. 5-6, 51)

4. **The Third Stage of UP polytheism: People will survive after death only by pleasing Pharaoh**

Survival after death seems always to have been of prime concern to the Egyptians. Insofar as they were truly convinced that their sole hope of immortality rested on the Pharaoh's good pleasure, it became easy for even a distant monarch to secure loyal and punctual obedience to his commands. Who would wittingly incur the god-king's wrath when penalties for disobedience were so drastic, and the rewards for good behavior seemed so sweet? Here, surely, lay the secret of the Old Kingdom. Instead of trying to control officials by law and frequent letters in Hammurabi's poor human fashion, the Egyptian Pharaoh could offer the reward of immortal life to those who obeyed him well. (McNeill, 1963, p. 74)

The contrast with Greece could not be greater, in geography, political power, and polytheism.

II. Greece

1. **Geography**

Early in their historical development, the inhabitants of the small steep valleys along the shores of Greece, perhaps in response to mounting population pressures, took to their ships in quest of other small and fertile valleys, where they founded new communities. *Moving by water, they enjoyed one possibility denied to growing areal societies.* Not only could they maintain regular communications with their new colonies, they could almost as easily exchange goods as messages, thus indefinitely extending the range of their economic base along the seacoasts. (Fox, 1971, p. 35; my italics)

The Greek landscape is that of the miniaturist—with rapid but never drastic transitions from valleys to hills and, for such a small country, with so many geographically distinct enclaves, including its many islands, that it is totally unlike the broader tract of plans and mountains that are characteristic of most other Mediterranean lands. *This simple geographic factor explains the separate development of the Greek city-states, which were bound by a common language and interest rather than by any sense of belonging to a distinct geographical entity*—until, that is, a sense of national unity was imposed on them from outside. *Greece's long coastline and the difficulties of land communication meant that seafaring always played an important part in Greek life and politics and probably contributed to the Greeks' readiness to explore the farther Mediterranean shores.* Unlike Asia Minor, or even Italy, Greece is a country of sea routes, not roads....

Something that may help explain why Greece emerged as a great civilization is the happy combination of geography and temperament: *a geographical location that permitted it to receive the benefits of the skills and resources of older civilizations and contemporary civilizations to the north, east, and south, and yet that was not especially vulnerable to attack by them*; and a spirit of inquiry, bred perhaps, in earlier generations of nomadic life, which was manifested by the Greeks' exploration, travel, and colonization and by a speculation about man and his world, which soon led to a sound basis for philosophical, political, and even scientific theory. Another important factor was a language that developed into the most subtle instrument for the expression of thought, science, and emotion that the West has known.

The achievements and legacy of Greek civilization can be assessed under many different heads, *and yet, the most significant contribution was probably an attitude of mind and an approach to political life* rather than works of art and literature. *The autocratic dynasties of the east and Egypt [UP] with their royal and priestly hierarchies could provide no model for politics in Greece. Instead the small kingdoms progressed* from system of rule by families or dictator (in the modern sense) *to rule by elected assemblies and councils and to recognition of the virtues of democracy,* as well as of its practical shortcomings. The practice of government came to be systematically analyzed for the first time, and the systems of different contemporary states compared. (Boardman, 1978, p. 324, my italics)

The inhabitants tended to cluster in the many highland or lowland plains, in river valleys, along the coastal strips backed by mountains, and on the scattered islands. Thus they formed a network of settlements of varied size and wealth, mostly separated by hills or sea from easy contact with each other. Throughout their history the Greeks have crossed these barriers continually; *but the geography fostered, though it did not alone create, an incandescent individualism* which made it hard for any Greek city-states to combine for long together.... *Each state developed politically at its own speed, worshipped its own concept of the Olympian gods*, spoke its own dialect of the common language, and wrote its own version of the common alphabet. (Jeffery, 1976, p. 23, my italics)

It is impossible to imagine Greek life without the sea. 'The wine-dark sea' pervades the work of Homer and he is adept at creating the feel of distance the Mediterranean, with all its hazards, puts between a returning exile and his home. In a land dominated by mountains it was the most obvious way of communication. It was far easier to cross the Aegean from west to east than to cross mainland Greece from east to west across the Pindus mountains. For heavy goods, in particular the metals which were lacking on mainland Greece itself and the luxury goods which the emerging aristocratic élite demanded, there was no other effective way of transport. This had been as true in the eighth century as it had been in Mycenaen times. *The sea also acted as a safety valve. It was the path of exile for Greeks fleeing as refugees in the twelfth century upheavals* and the gateway to new settlements as the populations of Greece outgrew the resources of their homeland in the eighth and seventh centuries. (Freeman, 1996, pp. 96-97; my italics)

So, while a Greek ship could go in every direction, to any island or hidden bay, an Egyptian ship could go only north or south along the Nile, on a single path easily controlled by pharaoh's navy, or his forts up or down the river with no escape through the desert, west or east.

Furthermore,

> The transition [to the *polis* in towns and cities] may have been easier because the aristocracy had no secure control over the local peasantries. There was, in fact, a deep-rooted prejudice against providing any form of regular labour for others. In Homer the landless labourer hiring himself out to others is presented as the lowest possible form of life, only marginally better than death. As a result the mass of the Greek population was never restricted in its mobility, and as population grew this made it possible for larger settlements, towns and cities, to emerge without hindrance, often through the merging of neighbouring villages. When they needed protection the farmers would retreat to local high ground [rare in Egypt]—the Acropolis in Athens, Acrocorinth in Corinth—but some Cycladic sites may have been walled as early as 900. (ib., p. 94)

2. DP Polytheism — The roots of the Greek religion

> Greek religion as it is currently understood probably resulted from the mingling of religious beliefs and practices between the incoming Greek-speaking people who arrived from the north during the 2nd millennium BC and the indigenous inhabitants whom they called "Pelasgi." The incomers' pantheon was headed by the Indo-European sky god variously known as Zeus (Greek), Dyaus (Indian), or Jupiter (Roman Diespater). But there was also a Cretan sky god...The incomers applied the name Zeus to his Cretan counterpart. In addition there was a tendency, fostered but not necessarily originated by Homer and Hesiod, for major Greek deities to be given a home on Mount Olympus. Once established there in a conspicuous position, the Olympians came to be identified with local deities and to be assigned as consorts to the local god or goddess. An unintended consequence (since the Greeks were monogamous) was that Zeus in particular became markedly polygamous. (Zeus already had a consort when he arrived in the Greek world and took Hera, herself a major goddess in Argos, as another).... At some date, Zeus and other deities were identified locally with heroes and heroines from the Homeric poems and called by such names as Zeus Agamemnon. (Pollard & Adkins, 2002, pp. 784-85)

To the invading Achaeans of c. 2000 BC, the gods were probably tribal, one god being the special protector of one tribe. On Olympus they began to lose their tribal associations, but they retained their preferences of the men or nations to whom they gave protection. (Michalopoulos, 1966, p. 58)

Within the Greek world picture the gods of Mount Olympus take a central place. The backgrounds of the individual gods are varied. Some are found in the Mycenaean Linear B tablets or have even earlier origins. Zeus, the father of the gods, is found in pre-Greek Indo-European cultures. Many other gods and goddesses are similar to those found in the Near East. Aphrodite, the goddess of love, has her equivalents in the Sumerian Inanna and the Semitic Astarte, and probably came to Greece from the Near East via Cyprus. Apollo's origins also appear to be non-Greek. Others may have had Greek roots but had absorbed attributes from the east. Typically, each god or goddess is a composite one, taking the final form from many different sources. (Freeman, 1996, p. 191)

3. DP Polytheism — The Homeric "DP Bible"

Homer exercised an enormous influence upon the religious development of later times—the famous statement that Homer and Hesiod created the Greek gods is as early as Herodotus—and this influence was exercised by the Homeric poems as completed whole, not while they were in the process of formation. Hence the justification from the point of view of the history of religion for treating Homer in the main as an undivided whole (Nilsson, 1980, p. 135)

The Homeric poems are pervaded from end to end by an elaborate polytheism. The *Iliad* begins with the anger of Apollo and ends with the gods conducting Priam to Achilles and ordering Achilles to yield to him the body of Hector. The *Odyssey* begins on Olympus and ends with the intervention of Athena which makes peace between Odysseus and the kinsmen of the slaughtered Suitors. Action on earth is accompanied by action, decision, and conflict in heaven, and gods and goddesses intervene in the human world. In the case of the *Iliad* the plot is held together by the constant agency of the divine, while Odysseus is brought home and defended by the goddess Athena; without her help he could not leave Calypso in the beginning, nor slay the Suitors in the end. In both poems the central characters draw what is, at least at one level, the moral of the whole story in terms of the gods. (Griffin, 1980, p. 144)

The gods play an essential part in the *Iliad* and the *Odyssey*. Homer presents them as a closely connected family with their home on Mount Olympus: Zeus and his wife Hera, their children, Ares, the god of war, and Hephaestus and, by Zeus' other liaisons, Apollo and Athena. However, they seldom work in unity. In the Odyssey Athena acts as a protecting goddess for Odysseus while Poseidon, Zeus' brother, is out to upset him. In the Iliad the gods are even more partisan. Hera and Athena are violently against the Trojans while Apollo takes their side. The gods can also act unscrupulously with each other to get their way. Hera tires Zeus with lovemaking so that she can put her own stratagems in hand while he is recovering in sleep. (Freeman, 1996, p. 92)

4. Multiplicitous polytheism

How could a pious Greek honour deities as diverse and mutually antagonistic as Artemis and Aphrodite? How was it possible for him to display his devotion to Aphrodite without denying the legitimacy of the claims of her personified antithesis? The answer surely has to do with the fact that mutual regard was not a necessary condition which determined whether men and gods did business together. Divided allegiance constituted the hallmark of polytheism and no man (or god) could be all things to all gods (or men). The very complexity of human life militated strongly against exclusive attachments. (Garland, 1992, p. 3)

III. Egypt, Decline and Fall

1. The pharaohs became ensnared in their own trap

The official cults in the great temples demanded more and more of the monarch's time and attention as the rituals in the vast temples increased in complexity with the development of the elaborate state religion. Under these circumstances the burden inevitably exceeded the powers of one man, even with the assistance of his vizier....In this decadent age the Pharaoh [Ramses IV] was more dependent upon such means [prayers placed in the mouth of Ramses III] for the maintenance of his power than upon his own strong arm....With fair promises of long reign the insatiable priesthood were exhorting from the impotent Pharaoh [Ramses IV] all they demanded while he was satisfied with the assured favour of the gods. The sources of that virile political life that had sprung up with the expulsion of the Hyksos were now exhausted. The vigorous grasp of affairs, which had once enabled the Pharaoh to manipulate with ease the difficult problems of the dominant oriental state, had now given way to an excessive devotion to religious works and superstitious belief in their effectiveness, which were rapidly absorbing every function of the state. Indeed, the state was rapidly moving toward a condition in which its chief function was religious and sacerdotal. (Breasted, 1948, pp. 236, 506-7).

2. The death of creativity

The key word for the developed spirit of this [last] period[20] was "silence," which we may render also with "calm, passivity, tranquility, submission, humility, meekness." (Wilson, 1979, p. 167).

> The desire to preserve the original purity of Egyptian culture eventually reached a stage of stagnation. The priests hid themselves away in a sterile research into rituals, adopting a concern for detail and complexity that came perilously close to Byzantinism (Grimal, 1992, p. 385)

> Did ancient Egypt contribute any significant element to the continuing philosophy, ethics, or world-consciousness of later times? No, not directly in fields which one may specify, as in the case of Babylonian science, Hebrew theology, or Greek or Chinese rationalism. One might critically say that the weight of ancient Egypt was not consonant with her size, that her intellectual and spiritual contributions were not up to her length

---

[20] The last dynasties (18th, 19th, 20th) before the Macedonian invasion.

of years and her physical memorial, and that she herself was unable to realize on her promising beginnings in many fields. (Wilson, 1979, pp. 167, 172)

> Egyptian techniques in working materials were in many respects different from those practiced elsewhere in the ancient world; artistic methods and conventions, established at the very beginning of the Dynastic Period, were quite peculiar to Egypt; even Egyptian writing, the hieroglyphic script, was a medium of communication developed specifically for the use of the tongue spoken in Egypt, and it was incapable of adaptation to the requirements of other languages. In techniques, art, and writing, the methods developed in the earliest times remained, in general terms, satisfactory for the needs of the Egyptian people and over the centuries required only the modifications resulting from natural development within a fairly closed culture. This self-sufficiency, which amounted almost to a sort of cultural stagnation, is well demonstrated in the matter of writing. When it became necessary to correspond diplomatically with other countries, the cuneiform script and the Akkadian language were used; this script, which was employed for many different ancient languages, displayed a versatility that Egyptian hieroglyphs never acquired. (James, 1978, p. 460)

"Tradition was an extremely important factor", as stressed by O'Connor (1983, p. 189) in his description of the Egyptian worldview, (1552-664 BC). However, an all-powerful tradition can easily become the precursor of ossification. Indeed, the "Late Period Egypt was afflicted by a 'Janusgesicht' (Janus head), a national schizophrenia characteristic of a culture in a state of advanced decay. In this view, Archaism reflected a deliberate effort to expunge the memories of the Third Intermediate Period; society was static and rigid;...At least partially, 'this culture was dying away from within' "(ib., p. 195).

Breasted (1948), pointed his finger in a different direction. For him,

> The situation is clear. A burst of military enthusiasm and a line of able rulers had enabled Egypt to assume for several centuries an imperial position, which her unwarlike people were not by nature adapted to occupy; and their impotent descendants, no

longer equal to their imperial role, were now appealing to the days of splendour with an almost pathetic futility. (p. 516)

But why put the blame on the "impotent descendants, no longer equal," when it is clear (e.g. from Breasted himself above) that the fault lay at the top of the pyramid: the unity of power, Pharaoh taking on the role of the omnipotent God? Why should the people be warlike if this presented no advantage, when everything stressed religion? Why be warlike if the system praised calm, passivity, tranquility, submission, humility, meekness?

It is instructive to note that the stronger the unity of power, the poorer the literature, and vice versa. Only in DP Greece could the high creativity of one author, Homer, have so great an impact on religion, literature, and ethnopsychology: a creativogenic impact which extends itself to our own times. And only in UP Egypt was the art of embalming bodies and ideas brought to such perfection that not one great writer existed or is known: in conditions similar to those of Byzantium and Venice.

6

The Decline and Fall of the Roman Empire

1. **In a nutshell**

   Over the first two centuries A.D. the ruling family transformed the Roman state into an imperial, oriental-style monarchy. By the third century, the emperor had come to resemble the ancient pharaohs. And it was the theocratic monarchy that was slightly modified for the Christian Roman Empire of the fourth century A.D. and perpetuated into medieval political life....As time went on, the role of the Senate became less and less important, and by the late empire, the law-making authority belonged to the emperor alone. At this point, Roman jurists proposed a legal theory, the *Lex Regia* (Royal Law), which stated that the legislative authority of the state once resided in the Roman people, but that the latter had surrendered this authority irrevocably to the emperor. Now the will of the emperor had the force of law. (Cantor, ib., pp. 7, 12)

2. **A special complex and complicated case**

   The causes and consequences of the fall of the Roman Empire in the West have been inexhaustible subjects of speculation and argument. (Cantor, 1993, p. 40)

   The causes of the fall of the empire have aroused a good deal of discussion. The reasons most often invoked are not definitive; the economic decline of the Roman world was not obvious in the 4th century, nor was the decay of the form of government or the defects of the administration. Nevertheless, the empire was yielding under the weight of its state superstructure and of taxation that was too heavy for the ancient world, where production and the standard of living were both very low. The army, which was extremely expensive, was not large enough; and even the population seemed to have declined [because of new diseases]. But it was really the massive invasions, which had become incessant during the second half of the century, that toppled the empire. (Petit, 1978, p. 1132)

Rome is a unique case because, for more than five-hundred years, it was a *DP* republic which only gradually became an *UP* empire. All the time, Rome's motto was SPQR, *Senatus Populusque Romanus* (The Senate and People of Rome), referring to the government of the ancient Roman Republic. The signature continued in use under the Roman Empire in which the emperors were considered the representatives of the people, even though the *senatus consulta*, or decrees of the Senate, were made at the pleasure of the emperor. Yet some form was respected: *Senatus Populusque Romanus* was inscribed on the arch of Emperor Titus (d. 81 AD), and SPQR on the arch of Emperor Septimius Severus (d. 211 AD).

Yet, the division of power of the Republic was incomplete, thereby explaining its limitations and lastly its transformation into a unity of power empire and final decline and fall.

3. Initially there was much practical but no major ideological *DP*, as between State and Church

Division of Power existed between the two consuls, and between them and the Senate and the Praetor, and the people but it was basically a social-political *DP* with everybody sharing the same philosophy:

> With the end of the monarchy [in 509 BC], a republican constitution gradually began to take form. The Romans' pragmatism led them to create a whole series of powers designed to balance one another while providing the maximum effectiveness to the essential proceedings of the state. Power was divided

among the Senate, the popular assemblies, and magistrates of varying degrees of importance.... The king's sovereign executive power appears to have passed initially to a magistrate with the title of *praetor maximus*, who no doubt headed a body of *praetores*, who had perhaps been the immediate officers of the monarch....The praetor maximus, however, soon gave way to a collegiate system in which two elected consuls shared the imperium for a single year. The principles of collegiality and of limitation of the term of office were characteristic of the republican constitution and effectively prevented the reappearance of tyrannical and absolute authority. (Bloch, 1998, p. 1087)

In the political life of republican Rome, the Senate constituted a third element, in addition to the popular assemblies and magistracies. Its prestige was great and its influence of continuing importance.....The Senate was originally composed of heads of the patrician gentes but soon came to include all former magistrates of the city, whose names were entered on the roll and who thus became *conscripti*.... The Senate's *auctoritas* manifested itself in all areas.... In the early centuries of the republic, the Senate thus had supreme influence, due to custom and to the respect in which it was held by the magistrates and popular assemblies. (Lindsay, 1978, p. 1088)

However, and this is important, Division of Power did not exist between Church and State (the *DP* that fosters individualism, critical thinking, innovation and high creativity) because in Rome, religion "was essentially a public religion. In contrast to the modern Western stress on private manifestations of religious commitment, religious observance in Rome consisted primarily in public or communal rituals and the interests of the gods were perceived to lie above all in the business of state, in political and military action." (Beard & Crawford, 1985, p. 30)

4. **Trend to absolute monarchy**

The early emperors usually made the Senate their mouthpiece and issued their laws in the form of senatorial decrees; by the 2nd century the emperor was openly replacing whatever other sources of written law had hitherto been permitted to function. After 100 A.D. the Assembly never met formally to pass a law, and the Senate often no longer bothered to couch its decrees in legal language, being content to repeat verbatim the speech with which the ruler had advocated the measure in question. After Hadrian, magistrates ceased modifying existing law by their legal interpretations because the praetors' *edictum perpetuum* had become a permanent code, which the emperor alone could alter. By 200, learned jurists had lost the right they had enjoyed since the time of Augustus of giving authoritative rulings on disputed points (*responsa prudentium*). (Petit, p. 1115)

5. **Imperial Bread and Circuses**

> *The public has long since cast off its cares; the people that once bestowed commands, consulships, legions and all else, now meddles no more and longs eagerly for just two things: panem et circenses - bread and circuses.*

    The Roman poet Juvenal (ca. AD 60-141) first made this famous statement in his Tenth Satire. Since then the quotation has been cited repeatedly as evidence of the decadence and irresponsibility of the population of Rome in the time of the Caesars. The author of the lines, however, was concerned less with fulminating against the games or the public distribution of grain than in condemning the Roman citizenry's lack of involvement in political life. The text describes the impotence of the people in the face of their autocratic sovereigns: the lethargy of those whom these sovereigns ruled and who, in Juvenal's opinion, had become mere non-political subjects....The circus offered a free mass spectacle to which everyone had access. The show was staged by the state itself, represented by the emperor or an official who made the arrangements for the game. (Köhne, 2000, pp. 8-9)

    The gladiatorial games form, indeed, the one feature of Roman society which to a modern mind is almost inconceivable in its atrocity. That not only men, but women, in an advanced period of civilization—men and women who not only professed but very frequently acted upon a high code of morals—should have made the carnage of men their habitual amusement, that all this should have continued for centuries with scarcely a protest, is one of the most startling facts in moral history. (Lecky, 1869/1955, p. 271)

6. Corruption

To a surprising degree, Roman imperial history resembles that of Han China.... Julius Caesar's (d. 44 B.C.) extralegal and almost nakedly military hold on the Roman state closely resembled the position Shih Huang-ti had won in China almost two centuries before. Moreover, both these upstarts set out to reorganize the power relations of their respective societies with scant regard for precedent or legal niceties; and their successors, after renewed bouts of civil war, found it prudent to veil naked military despotism behind more decorous forms....The Roman imperial bureaucracy under Augustus' successors suffered from ills similar to those besetting the Han—palace intrigue, systematically oppressive tax collection, and an occasionally corrupt officialdom. (McNeill, 1963, pp. 324-25)

McNeill's statement is corroborated by MacMullen in *Corruption and the Decline of Rome* of 1988, as summarized by Thomas Martin:

Over time, however, the application of power was gradually more and more privatized. That is, the wielders of power, whether bureaucrats or soldiers billeted among civilians, began routinely to exercise their power over others purely from private motives. Their overriding motive was profit. By the later Empire, everything official was for sale: honors, offices, tax breaks, exemptions from the military draft, and so on. Roman government had become one gigantic protection racket, with the army as its uncontrollable squad of goons.

The emperors could do little to correct this moral disaster because their exaggerated majesty kept them isolated from the world that they were supposed to govern. Since the palace staffs profited from their iron control of access to the ruler, they had every incentive to keep the emperors cut off from reality. Ultimately and most disastrously, pervasive corruption at all levels of administration undermined the physical security of the

Empire. Supplies and pay for the army were skimmed, commissions were bartered off to incompetents, recruitment were faked for profit. *In this way, the moral decline of Rome brought about the decline of its power as a state.* (1988, p. 7, my italics)

7. As foreseen by Lord Acton

This comment, that "the moral decline of Rome brought about the decline of its power as a state" could have been ascribed to Lord Acton, as discussed by Michael Grant in his *The Twelve Caesars*:

> Lord Acton, in the Appendix to his *Historical Essays and Studies,* wrote: 'Power tends to corrupt, and absolute power corrupts absolutely. Great men are always bad men.'...True, this sensational, almost unlimited, power was highly relevant—for another reason. It was not so much that it corrupted them after they had obtained it, but already, before that, it was what had tempted most of them to try to obtain the imperial office...And although absolute power, no doubt, sometimes proved a corrupting influence, Lord Acton might usefully, though less elegantly, have rewritten his assertion in the following terms: 'Overwork combined with fear tends to corrupt, and continual overwork and fear corrupt absolutely—with all the greater rapidity when combined with old age or ill-health.' (1975/2000, pp. 257-60)

These same corrupted Twelve Caesars[21] were discussed by Gore Vidal (1959):

> Other than the fact of power, the twelve Caesars as men had little in common with one another. But that little was significant: a fear of the knife in the dark. Of the twelve, eight (perhaps nine) were murdered. As Domitian remarked not long before he himself was struck down: "Emperors are necessarily wretched men since only their assassination can convince the public that the conspiracies against their lives are real."...
>
> Yet what, finally, was the effect of absolute power on twelve representative men? Suetonius makes it quite plain: di-

---

[21] Julius Caesar, Augustus, Tiberius, Caligula, Claudius, Nero, Galba, Otho, Vitellius, Vespasian, Titus, Domitian.

sastrous. Caligula was certifiably mad. Nero, who started well, became progressively irrational. Even the stern Tiberius's character weakened. In fact, Tacitus, in covering the same period as Suetonius, observes: 'Even after his enormous experience of public affairs, Tiberius was ruined and transformed by the violent influence of absolute power.' Caligula gave the game away when he told a critic, 'Bear in mind that I can treat anyone exactly as I please.' And that cruelty which is innate in human beings, now given the opportunity to use others as toys, flowered monstrously in the Caesars. (p. 637)

8. Emperors ruled in an atmosphere of almost unremitting fear and suspicion

"Excessive work and nagging fear, rather than absolute power, were the principal troubles which caused the Twelve Caesars, each in turn, to deteriorate" (Grant, 1975/2000, p. 258).

This almost unremitting fear and suspicion, suffered by nearly all emperors, is identified by Adrian Goldsworthy (2009) as the main cause of the decline and fall of the Roman Empire:

> Civil war and challenges to the imperial throne were common occurrences. Every adult emperor from Septimus Severus onwards experienced at least one such conflict during their lifetime. Usurpers never wanted to destroy or change the empire. These were not conflicts about ideology, but purely for political power.... Usurpers were the most direct and personal threat faced by any emperor and tended to be treated accordingly. It was normal for an emperor to abandon a war against a foreign enemy to deal with a Roman rival[22]....

---

[22] Note the parallel with an attempted (but failed) coup d'état tried on October 23, 1812 by General Claude François Malet, which was "a major factor in Napoleon's decision to hasten back [from Russia] ahead of the Grande Armée. Arriving in Paris on December 18, he proceeded to stiffen the dictatorship, to raise money and levy new troop" (Godechot, 1978, p. 836).

"Even more remarkable than the credulity of Malet's dupes [in accepting the false news of the death of Napoleon] was the submissiveness with which they accepted a change of regime, without even thinking of the empress or (their son) the king of Rome" (Herold, 1963, p. 325).

An emperor could not be everywhere at once. If he was unwilling to trust anyone else with sufficient power to deal with a distant problem, then it would simply not be dealt with at all. Time and again this sense of neglect by central government prompted a region to rebel and proclaim its own emperor.... All emperors lived with the fear of usurpation. It shaped their behavior and also that of all of the officials and officers who served under them. (pp. 401-11)

At a basic level the emperors and government officials of the Late Roman Empire had forgotten what the empire was for. The wider interests of the state—the *Res Publica,* or 'public thing', from which we get our word 'Republic"—were secondary to their own personal success and survival.... Emperors lived lives of fear, fully aware that they stood a good chance of meeting a sudden and violent death. Officials were equally nervous and suspicious of colleagues, as well as their imperial master (p. 418)

The Roman experience suggests that imperial decline is likely to start at the top. (p. 422, my italics)

9. Tuscans from the DP Republic of Florence could see it, already in the Early Renaissance

It was Ptolemy of Lucca (aka BartolomeoFiadoni, 1236-1327) who "had formed the clear-cut judgment that the power of Rome had been built under the consuls and free councils of the Republic, when 'no one among the Roman leaders wore a crown or was adorned with the purple, for his personal glorification.'" (Baron, 1955/66, pp. 55)

And it was Leonardo Bruni, humanist scholar and chancellor of the Republic of Florence (1427-44), who noted the negative

psychological impact of the Empire on the energies of the Roman people. The Republic, Bruni suggests, had seen eminent talents in every field of endeavor, but 'after the Republic had been subjected to the power of one man, those brilliant minds vanished, as Cornelius Tacitus says.' This judgment was something new—and something which until Bruni's day had been unimaginable—not only as an expression of humanistic and civic sentiment, but also because it rested on a new source of information. (ib., p. 58)

7

The DP Origins of Science

1. Introduction by way of contrast

Despite dozens of theories, the debate on the origin of Western science continues. Freeman Dyson recently gave an explanation attributing this origin to a unique European training in theological disputes.

According to Dyson:

> Western science grew out of Christian Theology. It is probably not an accident that modern science grew explosively in Christian Europe and left the rest of the world behind. A thousand years of theological disputes nurtured habits of analytical thinking that could also be applied to the analysis of natural phenomena.... There is nothing analogous to theology in Judaism or in Islam. I do not know much about Hinduism and Buddhism, but my Asian friends tell me that these religions have no theology. They have beliefs and stories and ceremonies and rules of behavior, but their literature is poetic rather than analytical. The idea that God may be approached and understood through intellectual analysis is uniquely Christian. (1998, p. 8)

While it sounds very interesting, is it valid? Definitely not in claiming an exclusivity of theological disputes for the West. A mere two months later, Dyson was corrected by Huston Smith (1998) who provided examples of major theological works by Jewish and Islamic scholars.

In the same vein, the present XIVth Dalai Lama explained in his autobiography that at the age of 24, before receiving his degree of Master of Metaphysics, he took examinations at three principal monastic universities of Tibet: "These examinations are always in the form of congregational debates.... At each of my preliminary examinations, I had to compete with fifteen learned scholars in these debates, three for each of the five treatises, and defend my thesis and refute their arguments.... [In all these debates the] arguments appear like battles of the intellect, which indeed they are" (1997, p. 27).

Furthermore, when reading from Dyson that "modern science grew explosively in Christian Europe" we must remember that for centuries "Christian Europe" included the Byzantine empire which, while far advanced in theological studies and debates, fell far behind in technological and scientific developments, notwithstanding that it had suffered less from barbarian invasions.

There is no doubt that quality disputes (philosophy, politics, history, theology) can nurture habits of analytical thinking; nevertheless it is hard to see why theological debates should have produced such different results in the West than elsewhere. It must be born in mind that results may depend on context: a context of division of power and freedom favoring the application of analytical thinking as opposed to the contrary within a context of unity of power. But, more importantly, division of power favors critical thinking which fosters the new. We therefore need a different theory on the origins of Western science.

Before proceeding, however, a major difference between the Christian East and the Christian West must be highlighted: the unity of power in the East and the division of power in the West. Judith Herrin, for instance, in her *The Formation of Christendom*, contrasted the Byzantine Patriarch Germanos [715-730] with his contemporary Pope Gregory II [715-731]:

> The main difference between the two church leaders remained the degree of secular control to which the Easterner was subjected. In the church of Constantinople, imperial interpretations of theology were as significant as patriarchal views, whereas in Rome the pope's definitions of doctrine were supreme. Conversely, the full authority of the Byzantine empire

could be put at the service of the orthodox, while the papacy had no comparable institution in Rome to give force to his sacerdotal leadership. Thus, popes were forced to manage the diplomatic affairs of central Italy and become political negotiators without material strength, and at the same time tried not to tolerate civilian pressure on the terrain of the spiritual. (1987, p. 341)

Even more to the point, Herrin wrote that "At every stage of his life, Germanos had witnessed the power of the emperor, just as his father had in a civilian capacity, and knew what it meant to oppose a Byzantine ruler.... [Because of this opposition, Germanos, as a youth] was castrated and forced into a clerical career" (p. 341).

In essence, what set apart the West from the Christian East, as well as from the rest of the world, was the division of power of the West; first between pope and emperor, then among king and parliament, and later between the executive, legislative and judiciary branches of the state.

What differentiated the West was first the humiliation of Emperor Henry IV at Canossa in 1077 at the hands of Pope Gregory VII, and then the humiliation of Emperor Frederick I Barbarossa at Venice in 1177 at the hands of Pope Alexander III, something that no Patriarch of Constantinople nor any other unarmed religious leader in the World ever dreamt to achieve.

2. In praise of technology

The contribution of theology to science might be debatable, but not so that of technology. This can be seen, for instance, in the following piece of advice which Galileo gave to all would-be scientists in his *Dialogues concerning Two New Sciences* of 1638:

> The constant activity which you Venetians display in your famous arsenal suggests to the studious mind a large field for investigation, especially that part of the work which involves mechanics; for in this department all types of instruments and machines are constantly constructed by many artisans, among whom there must be some who, partly by inherited experience and partly by their own observations, have become highly expert and clever in explanation. (1638/1914, p. 1)

Galileo appreciated technology because it was with the telescope, that he had manufactured in 1609 in his little workshop in Padua, "that began the most glorious phase of his scientific activity...the crowning of the practical ability he had acquired in his long years of close and intelligent manual work" (Geymonat, 1957, p. 56).

A similar praise for technology was made four hundred years earlier by Roger Bacon (1214-94) in his eulogy of Peter Peregrinus:

> Through experiment he gains knowledge of natural things, medical, chemical, indeed of everything in the heavens or earth. He is ashamed that things should be known to laymen, old women, soldiers, ploughman, of which he is ignorant. Therefore he has looked closely into the doings of those who work in metals and minerals of all kinds. He knows everything relating to the art of war, the making of weapons, and the chase. He has looked closely into agriculture, mensuration, and farming work. (Quoted by Woodruff, 1938, p. 47-48)

Peregrinus and Bacon had good reason to pay close attention to all kinds of manufacturing processes. As noted by Jean Gimpel, in *Medieval Machines:* "The Middle Ages introduced machinery into [Western] Europe on a scale no civilization had previously known. This was to be one of the main factors that led to the dominance of the Western hemisphere over the rest of the world" (1977, p. 1).

3. In praise of the technological contributions by Benedictine and Cistercian monks

The independence of a number of religious orders from the lay power structure allowed them to creatively pursue a broad range of activities:

> The waterwheel never played a major role in the Muslim world, not for lack of knowledgeability—Muslim hydraulic engineering was far ahead of European—but for want of fast-flowing streams. Large dams and intricate irrigation systems aided agriculture in Moorish Spain, but the waterwheel was used only for grinding grain and raising water. In Christian Europe, in contrast, the vertical wheel, including the powerful

overshot type, was finding important new applications. Once more the monasteries led the way. The great Benedictine abbey of St. Gall in Switzerland pioneered the use of waterpower for pounding beer mash as early as 900. The new Cistercian reform movement launched in 1098 at Citeaux, in Burgundy, carried on the Benedictine tradition of promoting technology by founding waterpowered grain mills, cloth-fulling mills, cable-twisting machinery, iron forges and furnaces (where the wheels powered the bellows), winepresses, breweries, and glassworks. The edge-runner mill, long known to China, was adopted for more efficient pressing of olives, oak galls and bark for tannin, and other substances requiring crushing.

The contemporary biographer of St. Bernard, leader of the Cistercian movement, illustrated the respect accorded the waterwheel; in describing the reconstruction of the saint's abbey of Clairvaux in 1136, he neglected the new church but included an enthusiastic account of the monastery's waterpowered machines. The first waterpowered iron mills in Germany, England, Denmark, and southern Italy were all Cistercian. (Gies&Gies, 1995, pp. 113-14)

Jean Gimpel, also, sang the praise of the monks:

The Cistercians, in their rapid expansion throughout Europe, must have played a role in the diffusion of new techniques, for the high level of their agricultural technology was matched by their industrial technology. Every monastery had a model factory, often as large as the church and only several feet away, and waterpower drove the machinery of the various industries located on its floor.... The Cistercians were always on the lookout for new techniques to increase the efficiency of their monasteries. (1977, p. 67)

The DP power structure around both the Benedictine and the Cistercian orders, including the granting of the foundation charter of the Benedictine Order of Cluny in 909 by Duke William of Aquitaine, *freed the abbey from all lay and local ecclesiastical jurisdiction and made it the property of Saints Peter and Paul, subject to no other authority but that of the pope.* The Cistercian monasteries were established on the poorest land, far from existing habitations, and strictly separated from the lay society. This freedom enabled the Benedictines to become champions of technological development. The monasteries, especially the Cistercian variety, were proto-Weberian capitalists, reinvesting all profits in an ever expanding cycle. This combination of freedom of action and proto-Weberian capitalism seem a better explanation for the technological success of the monks than their proficiency in theology.

Technological involvement by monks is unique to the West: nothing similar can be found in other civilizations, particularly not in those civilizations in which everything, to the smallest detail, is ruled by the unity of power of an emperor and his bureaucracy.

4.　The DP use of the clock by the West, and not by Byzantium

Probably few inventions prepared the mind to think more scientifically than the *democratic clock*. In the words of Daniel Boorstin:

> It was around 1330 that the hour became our modern hour, one of twenty-four equal parts of the day. This new 'day' included the night.... For the first time in history, an 'hour' took on a precise, year-round, everywhere meaning. There are few greater revolutions in human experience than this movement from the seasonal or 'temporary' hour to the equal hour. Here was man's declaration of independence from the sun, new proof of his mastery over himself and his surroundings.... By the fourteenth century in Europe large turret clocks in the belfries of churches and town halls were sounding the equal hours, heralding a new time-consciousness. Church towers, built to salute God and to mark man's heavenward aspirations, now became clock towers. The *torre* became the campanile" (1983, p. 39).

Western and Eastern Christianity had different attitudes toward the mechanical clock.

> [While in the West the Church,] signaled an acceptance of new technology and a readiness to compromise with new ideas, in the Greek Orthodox Church, there was no acceptance of new technology and no readiness whatsoever to compromise with new ideas. A remarkable demonstration of the strict obser-

vance of tradition in the Orthodox Church is given by the fact that until the twentieth century Orthodox priests never allowed a mechanical clock to be installed in an Orthodox church. For them it would have been blasphemy; for them the mathematical division of time and hours, minutes, and seconds had no relationship with the eternity of time. But the Church of Rome had no such objections to clocks being installed on the facade or towers of their churches, and today there are tens of thousands of mechanical church clocks in Western Europe. (Gimpel, 1977, p. 169-170)

Why the difference? Because the Western Church chose to fight the lay powers. A clock on a church tower provided a highly visible service to the community, in competition with the clock on the royal or communal palace. Besides the simple scanning of the time, the clock of the church told people that each of their actions, work or rest, had a spiritual value within God's redemptive scheme as administered by the Church. In the East, instead, where the Church was not able to establish its independence from the emperors, its only alternative was a policy of non-involvement and non-interference: a withdrawal from this world—including that of the exact measure of time.

The different attitudes toward the clock by Western and Eastern Christianity is but an aspect of the passion for *democratic technology* (in a climate of division of power), and the contrasting mild interest for *aristocratic technology* (under the unity of power). In the words of Carlo Cipolla, in the West, "Interest in the machine grew progressively stronger and was always characterized by those feelings of practicality and utilitarianism that prevailed in the medieval urban environment" (1967, p. 24). Byzantium, instead, when still technologically ahead of the West as its Roman heritage had been less destroyed by barbaric invasions, gave precedence to aristocratic applications of little consequence. Liudprand of Cremona who visited Constantinople in the year 949 saw, before the Emperor's seat, "a tree, made of bronze gilded over, whose branches were filled with birds, also made of gilded bronze, which uttered different cries, each according to its varying species" (ib., p. 25). The emperor sat on a throne which could be lifted rapidly, and in perfect silence, up to the ceiling, there to impress visitors (who had not seen it moving, while being prostrated in the initial greeting) with his infinite wisdom and might.

In the Byzantine empire—the land of the unity of power—technology had the task of amusing the great man, of showing off his power and wealth. In so doing, technologic and scientific development were strangled. The same happened in the West, any time that technology and science were diverted from practicality and utilitarianism and forced to serve the unity of power in any of its forms.

Five hundred years after Liudprand's visit, scientific development had stagnated so much that Cardinal Bessarion—in a report, addressed to Constantine Paleologos, ruler of the Byzantine province of Morea—recommended that a number of Constantine's best people be sent to the West to learn iron making, shipbuilding, mechanics, etc., with no attention given to the manufacture of glass and silk-weaving "which were devised for luxury and amusement" (ib., p. 28).

Specific to the present discussion is the praise given to the Byzantine civilization by Deno Geanakoplos who, after conceding that "no doubt the Byzantine contributions per se [to the West] were more passive and less creative in certain fields—for instance literature, philosophy, and science—..." stated that "there can be no doubt that the Byzantines were able to make truly original contributions, specifically in art and architecture; in forms of religious piety, the liturgy, and ecclesiastical literature; in aspects of philology; and perhaps not least, in providing the West something often overlooked by historians—a living example of a state with a highly centralized administration and tradition of statecraft under the rule of public law" (1976, p. 93). However, this overlooks the strong causal link between the power of a highly centralized administration and a passive and less creative role in literature, philosophy and science: all fields which demand freedom of thought and action. In contrast, as noted by Geanakoplos, Byzantium was creative in all the fields that prosper under a highly centralized administration, i.e. in the fields that in no way compete with the state: art (for icons), religious architecture, religious piety, liturgy, ecclesiastical literature, and philology. Indeed, who is the emperor, or high bureaucrat, who would complain if the intelligentsia concentrates its interest on purely religious matters?

In the West, the first clock striking equal hours was built, around 1335, for the church of Saint Gotthard in Milan: Milan which had been the backbone of the Lombard League which, with papal assistance, had defeated Emperor Frederick Barbarossa at Legnano in 1176. Equally indicative of the new spirit, and written between 1316 and 1321, is the first literary reference to a mechanical clock in a mostly religious yet highly politically committed poem: in Dante's[23] *Divine Comedy*, Paradise, Canto X.

5. China

What happened to the China which had "invented practically everything, aeons before anyone else" (Murphy, 1984, p. 187)? A strong bureaucratic government was the driving force behind everything, including the development of great technology, but with priorities which did not involve the public and the market place. What arose rapidly could just as quickly disappear under different state priorities, or be channeled along aristocratic tracks. Under such stilted conditions, the transition from technology to science was nearly impossible because even the intellectuals—the mandarins—were state bureaucrats under the orders of the unity of power. As Rhoads Murphy remarked, the

> urban merchants, the spearhead of change in the early modern West, were, in traditional China, too closely involved with and nurtured by the official system to fight against it. They had little to gain (unlike their Western counterparts) by upsetting the apple cart, either by changing the rules or by putting a new group in power. (ib., p. 193)

In China, the merchants did not upset the status quo, and technological development and science gradually stagnated. Both, John Merson and Joel Mokyr, pointed, very correctly in my opinion, to the changes at the top of the social pyramid:

> The Ming emperors [1368-1644] were also of a very different temper and type from the cosmopolitan and highly cultured rulers of the Song dynasty [960-1279]....The Ming were from the heartlands of rural China and, after two centuries of foreign

---

[23] Then, like the horloge, calling us to come,
What time the Bride of God doth rise and sing,
Wooing His love, her mattins to her Groom,

Where part with part will push and pull, and ring,
Ding-ding, upon the bell sweet notes that swell
With love the soul made apt for worshipping. (1316-21/1962, p. 139)

Mongol rule, a mood of xenophobia seemed to overcome both the court and the scholars who served it.... In 1433, and again in 1449 and 1452, imperial edicts banning overseas trade and travel, with savage penalties, were issued. Any merchant caught attempting to engage in foreign trade was defined a pirate and executed. For a time even learning a foreign language was prohibited as was the teaching of Chinese to foreigners.... Foreign contact, the only stimulus that might have provided change had been cut off and China's economic and cultural institutions were to remain, refined and perfected but, ultimately, out of step with what was taking place on the other side of the globe. (Merson, 1990, pp. 76-79)

The Ming and Qing [1644-1911] emperors were more absolute and autocratic than their predecessors. Before them, coups d'états and regicides occurred frequently, thus introducing an element of 'competition' into the Chinese political market. Rigid etiquette, complete obedience and conformism became the hallmark of the Chinese government under the Ming emperors. At the same time, the Chinese civil service became a major force in preserving the status quo. It learned to resist changes it did not want, and not even the most powerful emperors could implement progressive policies.... The absolutist rule of an all-powerful monarch whose preference was for stability above all discouraged the kind of dynamism that was throbbing throughout Europe at the time" (Mokyr, 1990, p. 237).

One seems to hear an echo of Byzantine history, of its emperors and its highly centralized administration; an echo of the adjective "byzantine" for structures and spirit characterized by complexity, deviousness and intrigue. China, instead of being on the forefront of technology and science, was found backward by Western visitors as early as the 16th century, not because of "biological aging", but because of monolithic governmental interference.

In China, aging occurred because little new was introduced and all proceeded as in the past; but the passing of time was not the cause for the aging. The passage of time could have brought improvements, as had happened in the past, and as was happening elsewhere.

On the other hand, one may ask why China was so extraordinarily creative for so long when ruled by imperial unity of power. To this question, Joseph Needham (1985) remarked that both China and Europe experienced feudalism, but that of China was of another kind:

> European feudalism was military-aristocratic ... [That of China was] very justifiably described as bureaucratic.... From the time of the first emperor, Ch'in Shih Huang Ti, onwards (third century BC), the old hereditary feudal houses were gradually attacked and destroyed, while the king or emperor (as he soon became) governed by the aid of an enormous bureaucracy, a civil service unimaginable in extent and degree of organization to the petty kingdoms of Europe. Modern research is showing that the bureaucratic organization of China in its earlier stages strongly helped science to growth; only in its later ones did it forcibly inhibit further growth, and in particular prevented a breakthrough which has occurred in Europe (p. 8).

Furthermore, I would add that the unity of power of the Chinese emperors was less unitary and less strong than that exercised by pharaohs, caliphs, Incas, and Byzantine emperors, because it was less theocratic; in other words religion played a different—one may say smaller—role in China than in Ancient Egypt, the Arab/Islamic countries, Peru, and the Byzantine empire. At any time in China, it was difficult to state concisely the main God and the corresponding religion. In the words of Laurence Thompson: "Chinese religion consists in the beliefs and practices of both the folk religious traditions and the great religious traditions of China (including Taoism, Confucianism, and Buddhism). Chinese religion may be regarded as essentially an expression of Chinese culture, rather than as several systems of dogma. The Chinese generally did not separate the religious from other aspects of their lives" (1978, p. 422). Thompson speaks of religious traditions, and not of religions with well defined gods. In conditions such as existed in China, the imperial power was more pragmatic and less dogmatic than in Ancient Egypt for instance, with a correspondingly less unitary shaping of the national scripts. Seen from a different angle, McNeill (1963) stressed how in China "The same individual might adhere to both philosophies [Confucianism and Taoism] with no sense of strain, since Confucianism was for public occasions, Taoism for private and personal moments. The anarchic, individualist emphasis of Taoism, which made Taoist organization something of a contradiction in terms, meant that the Chinese expressed in private the sentiments which other civilized societies incorporated into organized religion; and this may explain how Chinese government was able to maintain itself for more than two millennia without more than sporadic support from a public and emotionally powerful religion" (p. 313).

Both Joseph Needham (1985) and Robert Temple (1986) are right in stressing the major debt that Western technology and science owe to *The genius that was China* (to use the title of the 1990 book by John Merson). Yet this only increases one's interest in why the West, and not the Arab-Islamic Empire, or the Byzantine Empire for instance, became the inheritor to the Chinese discoveries. Once again, much of what prospered under the stimulus and protection of the bureaucracy died when the emperors became more powerful and the bureaucracy ossified.

6. The papal DP contribution to the independence of the first universities 1200 →

The universities also profited from the *War of Supremacy* between the papacy and the lay powers, and devoted themselves to teaching science and fostering technological and scientific development. One hundred and thirty-seven years after Canossa, as reported by Jacques Le Goff,

> [at] Oxford, thanks to the excommunicated John Lackland's eclipse of power, the university obtained its first liberties in 1214.... [It was] a legate of Innocent III, Cardinal Nicholas of Tusculum who granted the beginning of the university's independence. Against Henry III, Pope Innocent IV placed it 'under the protection of St Peter and the Pope,' and ordered the bishops of London and Salisbury to protect it against royal schemes. [Earlier], in 1194 in Paris, Pope Celestine III granted the [university] corporation its first privileges, and it was primarily Popes Innocent III and Gregory IX who assured its autonomy. In 1215 the papal legate, Cardinal Robert de Courçon, gave the university its first official statutes. In 1231, Gregory IX, who accused the bishop of Paris of negligence and forced the king of France and his mother to give in, granted new statutes to the university

through the famous bull *Parens scientiarium*, which has been called the university's 'Magna Carta'. (1993, p. 68-70)

The papal strategy was clear: freedom for the universities, from kings and local bishops, meant more power for the popes. Yet, for science, it provided the beginning of real freedom. For the universities, freedom was the true "Parent of the sciences" as said in the title of the bull of 1231. Such an intervention by the church in the affairs of the state—bolstered by a war of supremacy between popes and emperors/kings, and derived division of power—would have been inconceivable in China where even astronomy and the calculation of the calendar were the strict prerogatives of the emperor and his government. Such prerogatives meant control over both the past and the future, ensuring that the future did not bring revolutions but a calm repetition of the past.

7. The discovery of the individual 1080-1200

That the beginning of a new way of thinking coincided with the *Investiture Controversy* (1075-1222), had already been remarked by Colin Morris in his *The Discovery of the Individual 1050-1200* when he wrote that: "There is a rapid rise in individualism and humanism from about 1080 to 1150" (1972, p. 7), an individualism truly unique to the West: "The Asiatic and Eastern tradition of thought has set much less store by the individual than the West has done. Belief in reincarnation virtually excludes individuality in the Western sense, for each person is but a manifestation of the life within him, which will be reborn, after his apparent death, in another form. Western individualism is therefore far from expressing the common experience of humanity. Taking a world view, one might almost regard it as an eccentricity among cultures" (ib., p. 2).

8. The shift to quantification 1250-1350

Alfred Crosby, in his *The Measure of Reality* of 1997 wrote how between 1250 and 1350,

> a marked shift occurred in the West, from qualitative perception to, or at least toward, quantification perception....The West lacked firmness of political and religious and, speaking in the broadest generality, cultural authority. It was, among the great

civilizations, unique in its stubborn resistance to political, religious, and intellectual centralization and standardization.... Western Europe was a warren of jurisdictions - kingdoms, dukedoms, baronies, bishoprics, communes, guilds, universities, and more - a compost of checks and balances. Not authority, not even the vicar of Christ on earth, had effective political, religious, or intellectual jurisdiction... [In contrast] The political and religious aristocracies of Asia and North Africa always ultimately united to keep the nouveau riche down. In the West, on the other hand, merchants and bankers even managed to establish their own family dynasties and to insinuate themselves into political prominence; most famous, of course, were the Medici, but there were also the Fuggers and a goodly number of lesser lineages of wealth and influence. Money changers were the yeast that the lump—peasant, priest, or noble—never could evict or sterilize, and that quickened and even recruited among the traditional classes. (pp. 54-55)

Crosby also identified the division of power of the West, in contrast with the unity of power of the Far-East, East and South: a division of power which led to the "West's distinctive intellectual accomplishment [of bringing] mathematics and measurement together and to hold them to the task of making sense of a sensorial perceivable reality" (ib., p. 17).

9. A passion for mechanization 1200 →

In the words of Carlo Cipolla (1994):

One of the original features of western technological development after the twelfth century was the increasing emphasis placed on the mechanical aspects of technology. There was a real passion for the mechanization of all productive processes. In the Forez by 1251, there existed a mill to grind mustard, and by the end of the Middle Ages mechanical clockwork had been successfully applied to the roasting of meats. The basic reason for this attitude is not easy to grasp. One may argue that the shortage of labor brought about by repeated epidemics favored the adoption of labor-saving devices, but a phenomenon by its nature so complex can scarcely be reduced to naive and simplistic determinism.

Necessity explains nothing; the crucial question is why some groups respond in a particular way to needs or wants which in other groups remain unformulated and unfilled. (pp. 150-51)

10. The discovery of the human body through public dissections 1315 →

The use of dissection (autopsy) of dead human bodies for research is what differentiates Western medicine from the healing and curing approaches of the other civilizations. Because of this fundamental difference, the practice of dissection of humans deserves to be seen as the real beginning of Western medicine: *"The Greatest Benefit to Mankind"*.

Without dissections, it is not possible to understand how the human body is made, how it functions, and how it can be repaired and cured. The prohibition of dissection in other civilizations has been one of the primary reasons for their lack of medical progress, beyond some very promising beginnings.

Roy Porter titled his 1997 medical history of humanity: *The Greatest Benefit to Mankind*. However, without scientific research, this benefit would have remained limited. In the words of Benjamin Gordon: "The lack of scientific knowledge bound medical practice to superstition, to the beliefs in amulets, and to the reliance on herb decoction, astrology, and uroscopy" (1959, p. 592).

"Because Hindus were prohibited by their religion from cutting the dead body, their knowledge of anatomy was limited" (Underwood & Rhodes, 1993, p. 776). Not only were Hindus so restricted, but so were the Jews, the Muslims, and the Byzantines.

Among the Jews: "Respect for the dead, and the utmost reverence for the human body after death are enjoined by both Jewish law and custom. The rabbis deduce the prohibition of the desecration of the corpse as well as the duty of the reverent disposal of the body by burial as soon as possible after death from Deuteronomy 21:22, 23. Mutilation of the body, whether for anatomical dissection or for post-mortem examination, would appear to violate the respect due to the dead, and is consequently to be forbidden" (Rabinowitz, 1971, pp. 932-33).

In Byzantine medicine, "Great stress, almost to the point of worship, was laid on ancient tradition. The medicine of Galen (Claudius Galenus, ca. 130-200 A.D.) and other ancient physicians (as interpreted by the church of course) was considered the last word on the subject of medicine. Independent thought was considered a heresy even by physicians themselves.... Byzantine medicine, to be exact, is a mechanical preservation of ancient thought or an anthology of the classical medical writings" (Gordon, 1959, p. 44). In these conditions, any thought of proceding beyond the dissections of animals as practiced by Galen would have been anathema.

In the Islamic countries, "The theory and thought of the Greeks were left untouched and treasured up after careful systematization and classification. It must be remembered that the Muslims were strictly prohibited from dissecting either human bodies or living animals. Thus experiment was practically impossible in medicine, so that none of Galen's anatomical and physiological errors could be corrected" (Meyerhof, 1931, p. 344).

The scientific study of the human body through dissection was unique to the West for a long time. Among the pioneers, two names stand out: those of Mondino de' Luzzi, and Andrea Vesalius.

>The first recorded public human dissection was conducted in Bologna around 1315 by Mondino de Luzzi (c. 1270-1326).... His fame rests on his *Anatomia Mundini* (c. 1316), which became the standard text on the subject. Built on personal experience of human dissection, the *Anatomia* was a brief, practical guide, treating the parts of the body in the order in which they would be handled in dissection, beginning with the abdominal cavity, the most perishable part (Porter, 1997, p. 132).

In 1315, the year of the first public dissection by Mondino, Christianity had no pope. The Holy See, already forced to move to Avignon, was vacant from 1314 to 1316. The French members of the college of cardinals, who out-numbered the Italians, were unable to agree on a pope. Finally they agreed on another Frenchman, Jacques Dréze de Cahous, who reigned as John XXII from 1316-1334 after Clement V (1305-1314).

After Mondino's disections in 1315, others followed: public dissections were instituted at the Universities of Montpellier in 1377, of Catalonia Lerida in 1391, Padua in 1429, Prague in 1460, Paris in 1478, and Tübingen in 1485. Dissections by Leonardo da Vinci followed shortly after in 1507-08.

> On another anatomical page dated c. 1508 he claims to have personally dissected—*disfatto:* taken to pieces—more than ten human bodies. He boasts of his finesse with the scalpel.... In terms of what he actually contributed—of the difference he made—his work as an anatomist is far more significant than his work as an engineer, or inventor, or architect. He mapped and documented the human body more rigorously and specifically than had been done before; his anatomical drawings constituted a new visual language for describing body-parts, as his mechanical drawings did for machines. There is a certain dogged courage in these investigations, which were beset by taboos and doctrinal doubts, and which depended on the stressful and repulsive procedures of post-mortem examination in pre-refrigeration circumstances. Leonardo's anatomy exemplifies his belief in practical, empirical, hands-on investigation.... Leonardo's anatomical studies belong under the heading 'Leonardo the scientist', but are also vitally connected with Leonardo the artist: they bridge the gap between those roles, or show that it is not really a gap at all. Anatomy was one of the building blocks of painting, like geometry and mathematics. (Nicholl, 2004, p. 422, 240-1)

> Perhaps the most famous of Leonardo's anatomical drawing is this one of a fetus inside the womb. Faulty as it is in some respects, in others—notably the position of the fetus and umbilical cord—it is so accurate and so expertly drawn that it can still be used as an example in medical textbooks today....Leonardo's great contribution to anatomy lay in the creation of a system of drawing, still in general use, which enabled physicians to trans-

mit their findings to students.... With the appearance of the first "modern" medical textbook, the *De humanis corporis fabrica* of Vesalius (1543), which was illustrated with woodcuts based on Leonardo's method, anatomical drawing became what it is today. (Wallace, 1967, pp. 103-05)

11. Of so many important factors, remember one: The public dissections of Mondino de Luzzi

The technological contributions by the Benedictine and Cistercian monks to the birth of Western science were important, as was the papal contribution to the independence of the first universities. The use of the clock, a passion for quantification and mechanization, and the discovery of the individual were also very important. Yet to be remembered for their relevance to our times are the public dissections 1315 → because without them there would be no scientific medicine—the key element of *The greatest benefit to mankind*—and no real freedom from the world of mysteries.

8

Conclusions

1. Truth

In *Objective Knowledge* Karl Popper said: "I accept the common-sense theory (defended and refined by Alfred Tarski) that truth is the correspondence with the facts (or with reality); or more precisely, that a theory is true if and only if it corresponds to the facts" (1975, p. 44). This, too, is my position.

But when can we ever fully know Truth? When can we be certain that a test, even if repeated successfully many times, will say something valid about reality? My answer is: when the new discovery fits within a major web of different, well tested pieces of knowledge, which are theoretically integrated, and lead to fully confirmed original forecasts.

One good example of this comes from the 1616 work of William Harvey in discovering of and giving full evidence for the circulation of blood:

> He had not only furnished himself with all the knowledge that books and the instructions of the best anatomists of Italy could give, but, by a long series of dissections, had gained a far more complete knowledge of the comparative anatomy of the heart and vessels than any contemporary had. Thus equipped, he began his investigations into the movements of the heart and blood by seeing their action in living animals. He minutely describes what he saw in dogs, pigs, serpents, frogs and fishes, and even in slugs, oysters, lobsters and insect, in the transparent shrimp, and lastly in the chick while still in the shell. He

particularly describes his observations and experiments on the ventricles, the auricles, the arteries and the veins.... He elaborately and clearly demonstrates the effect of obstruction of the bloodstream in arteries or in veins, by the forceps in the case of a snake, by a ligature on the arm of a man, and illustrates his argument by figures. These results can be explained only by the constant circulation of the same blood (Pye-Smith & Singer, 1973, p. 143)

What I say in this chapter, on the impact of power united or divided, does not fully meet the Tarskian definition of truth, nor does it include as many tests as Harvey's, but it comes very near to a "correspondence with the facts" and a "well tested piece of knowledge, theoretically integrated, and leading to confirmed original forecasts."

2. Importance

All civilizations, and individual nations, deserve great praise for the creativity of their DP youthful centuries. This applies in particular to the civilization with the highest division of power. There is no need to describe the continuous high level of creativity in the West in science, philosophy, and the arts. What must be highlighted is its high creativity, especially in the last centuries, in the most important fields of law, morality, humanitarian help, and peace. This includes the abolition of slavery and torture, reduction in racial, ethnic, gender prejudice; the foundation of the Red Cross in 1864 by Henry Dunant, and the creation by Alfred Nobel, at the turn of the century, of five yearly prizes, including one for peace. Then followed, through worldwide cooperation, the creation of the League of Nations in 1919, United Nations in 1945, UNICEF in 1946, the proclamation of the Universal Declaration of Human Rights in 1948, and Amnesty International in 1961.

3. Division of Power from Theory, Unity of Power from Force

It is important to stress how the division of power runs counter to nature, which leans more towards the unity of power, so that some powerful thinking is required to identify the many benefits proffered by DP and the basic faults of the UP.

The Unity of Power easily wins with its force and first results:

> As the German emperor Henry III [r. 1039-1056] put it, rather crudely, in the mid-eleventh century: 'For those who govern laws are not governed by laws, since the law, as they commonly say, has a nose of wax, and the King has an iron hand, and a long one, and he can bend the law in whatever way it pleases him.' Who had the supreme court—king and emperor, or pope? Who could judge and depose whom? It was the same as asking who was the head of the body: the argument was circular. And since it could not be resolved by argument it was, in practice, determined by the balance of force.
>
> Until the latter part of the eleventh century, the balance lay heavily with the secular arm. Charlemagne had sat in judgment on the Pope, Leo III, and confirmed him in office after trial. In a letter to Leo, which has survived, he treats him, quite unambiguously, as merely the chief of his bishops. And bishops were royal functionaries. (Johnson, 1976, p. 192)

In our times, the world has suffered from the "natural UP" of the *Führerprinzip*, as promulgated in 1925 by Hitler himself in *Mein Kampf*:

> Since the folkish state is to be based "on the aristocratic idea of nature" it follows that democracy is out of the question and must be replaced by the *Führerprinzip*. The authoritarianism of the Prussian Army is to be adopted by the Third Reich: "authority of every leader downward and responsibility upward."
>
> There must be no majority decisions, but only responsible persons... Surely every man will have advisers by his side, but the *decision will be made by one man.* ...only he alone may possess the authority and the right to command....It will not be possible to dispense with Parliament. But their councilors will then actually give counsel...In no chamber does a vote ever take place. They are working institutions and not voting machines. This principle—absolute responsibility unconditionally combined with absolute authority—will gradually breed an elite of leaders such as today, in this era of irresponsible parliamentarianism, is utterly inconceivable. (quoted by Shirer, 1960, pp. 89-90).

Praise for the Division of Power comes from powerful theoreticians of the caliber of Humbert of Silva Candida, Dante and Montesquieu:

Humbert of Silva Candida

The moving spirit behind the *Investiture Controversy* of 1075-1122 and the 1077 humiliation of Emperor Henry IV at Canossa at the hand of Pope Gregory VII was Humbert, first monk at Cluny, then Abbot of Moyenmoutier and Cardinal Bishop of Silva Candida,

> The ideas which inspired his activity are to be seen in his treatise *Against the Simonists* (ca. 1058), which is at once the earliest, the ablest, and the most extreme statement of the programme of the reformers. To Humbert, simony was not merely a sin; it was the supreme heresy, since it denied the spiritual character of the Church and subordinated the gifts of the Spirit to money and worldly power. But since the Holy Ghost cannot be bought or sold, it follows, so he argued, that the Simonists had no share in His gifts. Their sacraments were null and void, and their church was the church of Anti-Christ. To meet these evils he called for a return to the old canonical principles of free election and the emancipation of the Church from the control of the secular power and from the custom of lay investiture. Since the spiritual power is as superior to that of the king as heaven is superior to earth, the Church should guide and rule the state as the soul rules the body; so only was it possible to ensure the reign of justice and the peace and union of the Christian people.
>
> It is clear that these views are irreconcilable, not only with the current practice and union of eleventh-century Feudalism, but with the whole tradition of the imperial state Church which had inextricably confused spiritual and secular functions, and had regarded emperors and kings as the divinely appointed leaders of Christian society. (Dawson, 1950/1964, p. 51)

Dante

Dante is the great precursor of the modern theoreticians of the division of power[24] with his *Monarchia*, in which he states that the imperial authority depends directly on God, and not on his vicar, the pope, to whom, nonetheless, the sovereign owed filial reverence. For Dante, there must be cooperation between the two supreme powers

---

[24] "Dante's exceptional ability for probing a question to its causal origins enables him to produce a solution for the problem of how a universal authority, once it is established, can be controlled. This he does by dividing the authority according to the two goals of humanity and defining their areas of responsibility" (Anderson, 1980, p. 223).

because both are necessary: one to achieve terrestrial happiness, the other the celestial one.

> The *Monarchia* had a profound influence in its century; it was revised and used by the supporters of Lewis of Bavaria in his propaganda against the papacy; and it even influenced the Golden Bull of 1356, whereby the emperor Charles IV, the grandson of Henry VII, came to an accord with the electors of the empire; it was so feared by the opposing party that it was condemned by the Dominican friar Guido Vernani, was burnt in public at Bologna in 1329, and was placed on the *Index* when emperor Charles V used it in his quarrels with the papacy. Its arguments were taken up by Protestant writers in the sixteenth century, most notably by Bishop Jewel and John Foxe, the author of the widely influential *Boke of Martyrs* [1563]. (Anderson, 1980, p. 224)

Montesquieu

> But it was Montesquieu, above all, who made clear that this principle of the separation of powers was indeed the distinguishing feature of the British Constitution, Lords, Commons, and Crown, each restraining the other, the judiciary independent, all the interests of the Kingdom beautifully balanced in the process, and liberty rising triumphant from it all. How discerning of Montesquieu to see this, and how wise of the British thus to fragment political power in order to frustrate tyranny. And what an incalculable debt Americans owed to Montesquieu, and to the Mother Country, for setting so improving an example to them, and to the rest of the world. How odd, too, that with all these limitations on the abuse of power, it should have been necessary for the Americans to revolt! ....

> The principle that inspired separation of powers may have been doctrinaire, but there was nothing doctrinaire about the energy of a Washington or the audacity of a Hamilton or the authority of a Marshall.... Madison's observation that ultimate reliance must be not on "external principles" but on the "internal structure" of government was profound, but even it did not penetrate to the heart of the matter. *Ultimate* reliance was on the virtue, the intelligence, and the sophistication of the people.

This was not wanting in the Revolutionary generation. (Commager, 1977/2000, pp. 217-18, 255)

Montesquieu was not only the spirit behind the power separation articles of the Constitution ("Nearly all of America's political leaders were familiar with the writings of the Baron Montesquieu" noted Richard Beeman in *Plain, Honest Men: The making of the American Constitution*), but he was used to gain the ratification of the basic text of the Constitution, as submitted to the 13 States on September 28, 1787. James Madison in the *Federalist* paper 47 of February 1, 1788, wrote that:

> The famous Montesquieu is the political theorist most often cited on this subject. If he is not the author of the principle of separation of powers, he can at least be credited with being its most effective and outspoken supporter, having brought it to the attention of the rest of mankind. Therefore, it's worth trying to understand his basic ideas on this subject....The reasons which Montesquieu himself provides us with to back up his political principles make his intentions even more clear:
>
> *When the legislative and executive powers are united in the same person, or in the same body of magistracy, there can be then no liberty; because apprehensions may arise, lest the same monarch or senate should enact tyrannical laws, to execute them in a tyrannical manner....were the power of judging joined with the legislative, the life and liberty of the subject would be exposed to arbitrary control, for the judge would then be the legislator. Were it joined to the executive power, the judge might behave with all the violence of an oppressor.*
>
> Montesquieu explains some of these things in more detail in other passages, but even from this short passage it is clear what this famous political theorist actually meant when he was discussing the great political principle of separation of powers. (1788/2011, p. 300)

Therivel's Volunteering as the Ultimate Division of Power

Moral individualism and volunteerism are the logical extension of the division of power between papacy and empire, between king and parliament, between executive, legislative and judiciary powers. They are its logical extension by which every individual—through active participation in several voluntary associations—acquires knowledge, power and wisdom and feels responsible for society in general, and for specific groups of people or issues. Indeed, "voluntary organizations point with great pride to their independence and to their ability to innovate and experiment.... But most importantly, they are the primary mechanisms through which citizens get involved in the life of their communities. That involvement can empower citizens, can solve pressing community problems, can build a sense of interdependence and mutual responsibility. That involvement is the surest balance against the domination by the government, business or any other force that seeks to subvert the public interest to its own ends" (Allen 1982, pp. 108-09).

"Empowering the citizens" is what gives volunteerism its universal value, its authentic democratic essence. Volunteerism is more than casting a vote every two years, it is active generous participation, in cooperation with others, acquiring jointly the know-how and the right to prod and criticize the work of federal and local authorities and to propose better ways to assist people and solve difficulties. This praise is not only the logical extension of a theory which extols the virtues of the division of power, but the recognition that individual morality—when incarnated in the new volunteerism—is the ideal form of self-actualization and happiness, as pointed out by Baden-Powell, the founder of the Scout Movement: "There is only one success in life, and that is Happiness; and true happiness comes out of service" (quoted by Jeal, 1989, p. 516).

And the same was stressed by the great Indian poet Rabindranath Tagore:

> I slept and dreamt that life was joy.
> I awoke and saw that life was service.
> I acted and behold, service was joy.
> (quoted by Goswami, 1993, p. 195).

So:

Volunteerism for the ultimate success in life, happiness;
Volunteerism for joy through service;
Volunteerism to make a difference[25];
Volunteerism to be great[26];
Volunteerism to change the world[27],

and

Volunteerism to empower everybody in a full division of power which takes cognizance of past history (China, Egypt, Rome, Byzantium, Arab World, Nazi Germany, the history of science [medicine in particular] and the contribution of the great theorists of the division of power.

"*Division of power*" speaks of opposing or at minimum of contrasting "division" and not of mild "separation," and of "power" and not of "powers" as in *separation of powers*. "Division of power" stimulates critical thinking much more than "separation of powers": that critical thinking implied by Commager in *The Empire of Reason* when he stressed that the "*Ultimate* reliance was on the virtue, the intelligence, and the sophistication of the people. This was not wanting in the Revolutionary generation[28] [and in all good DP generations]."

---

[25] "Hillary [Clinton] did the things she did because she wanted to make a difference" (Clinton, 2007, p. xi).
[26] "Martin Luther King once said, 'Everyone can be great because everyone can serve" (quoted by Clinton, 2007, p. xiii).
[27] From the title of Bill Clinton's 2007 *Giving: How each of us can change the world*, which describes the present explosion of citizen service: "Since the end of the Cold War, for the first time in history a majority of the world's people are living under [DP] elected governments, which create more opportunities for democratic societies and citizen activism to develop. And because of the global mass media culture and leaders' unavoidable sensitivity to public opinion, even nondemocratic governments find it increasingly difficult to prevent people from organizing for advocacy or action. When I became president in 1993 there were virtually no NGOs in Russia or China. Today, even though President Vladimir Putin has severely restricted them, Russia has more than 400,000. China has almost 280,000 NGOs registered with the government, and perhaps twice that number unregistered. India, a democracy born out of Gandhi's citizen activism, has more than 500,000 working NGOs. The United States has more than one million charitable organizations, twice as many as in 2000. They employ 10.2 million people, 7 percent of our workforce." (p. 9)
[28] Following a line of development that started in Canossa, 1077, moved to Cambridge 1174, Runnymede 1215, and Plymouth Rock 1620.

References

Allawi, Ali A. (2009). *The crisis of the Islamic civilization*. New Haven, CT: Yale University Press.

Allen, Kerry K. (1982). Social responsibility: The growing partnership of business and voluntary organizations. In J.D. Harman (Ed.), *Volunteerism in the eighties: Fundamental issues in voluntary action* (pp. 95-110). Landham, MD: University Press of America.

Anderson, Mary M. (1990). *Hidden power.The palace eunuchs of imperial China*. Buffalo, NY: Prometheus.

Anderson, William (1980). *Dante the maker*. London: Routledge&Kegan Paul.

Baden-Powell, Robert, S. (2001). *Footsteps of the founder: The Baden-Powell quotation book*. Rome: Edizioni Scout.

Balazs, Etienne (1964). *Chinese civilization and bureaucracy*. New Haven, CT: Yale University Press.

Baron, Hans (1955/1966). *The crisis of the early Italian Renaissance*. Princeton, NJ: Princeton University Press.

Beard, Mary, & Crawford, Michael (1985). *Rome in the late Republic.* Ithaca, NY: Cornell University Press.

Beeman, Richard (2009). *Plain, honest men: The making of the American Constitution*. New York: Random House.

Berendt, John (2005). *The city of falling angels*. New York: Penguin Press.

Berlin, Isaiah (1953/1667). *The Hedgehog and the Fox*. London: Weidenfeld and Nicolson.

Bloch, Raymond (1998). Rome from its origins to 264 BC. In *Encyclopaedia Britannica, (15,* pp. 1085-91). Chicago: Encyclopaedia Britannica.

Boardman, John (1978). Ancient Greek civilization. In *Encyclopaedia Britannica (8,* pp. 324-34). Chicago: Encyclopaedia Britannica.

Boorstin, Daniel J. (1983). *The discoverers: A history of man's search to know his world and himself.* New York: Random House.

Bouwsma, William J. (1973/1990). Venice and the political education of Europe. In his *A usable past: Essays in European cultural history* (pp. 266-91). Berkeley: University of California Press.

Breasted, James H. (1948). *A history of Egypt.* London: Hodder & Stoughton.

Byron, Robert (1929). *The Byzantine achievement: An historical perspective A.D. 330-1453.* New York: Alfred A. Knopf.

Cantor, Norman (1993). *The civilization of the Middle Ages.* New York: HarperCollins.

Chang, Pang-Mei, Natasha (1997). *Bound feet & Western dress.* New York: Bantam Books.

Cipolla, Carlo M. (1967). *Clocks and culture 1300-1700.* New York: Walker.

Cipolla, Carlo (1994). *Before the Industrial Revolution: European society and economy, 1000-1700.* New York: W. W. Norton.

Clinton, Bill (2007). *Giving: How each of us can change the world.* New York: Alfred A. Knopf.

Commager, Henry Steele (1977/2000). *The Empire of Reason: How Europe imagined and America realized the Enlightenment.* London: Phoenix Press.

Crosby, Alfred W. (1997). *The measure of reality.* Cambridge: Cambridge University Press.

Dalai Lama [14th] (1997). *My land and my people: The original autobiography of His Holiness the Dalai Lama of Tibet.* New York: Warner.

Dante, Alighieri (1316-21/1962). *The Divine Comedy - Paradise.* London: Penguin Books.

Dawson, Christopher (1950/1964). Monastic reform and Christian culture. In W. Schafer (Ed.), *The Gregorian epoch* (pp. 47-54). Boston: D.C. Heath.

Dennis, George T. (1997). Imperial panegyric: Rhetoric and reality. In H. Maguire (Ed.), *Byzantine court culture from 829-1204* (pp. 131-40), Washington, D.C.: Dumbarton Oaks Research Library and Collection.

Diehl, Charles (1949). Byzantine Art. In N.H. Baynes & H. St.L.B. Moss (Eds.), *Byzantium: An introduction to East Roman civilization* (pp. 166-99). Oxford: Clarendon.

Diehl, Charles (1957). *Byzantium: Greatness and decline.* New Brunswick, NJ: Rutgers University Press.

Dyson, Freeman J. (1998, May 28). Is God in the Lab? *New York Review of Books,* 8-10.

Ebrey, Patricia B. (1993). *The inner quarters: Marriage and the lives of Chinese women in the Sung Period* [960-1279]. Berkeley: University of California Press.

Emery, Walter B. (1961). *Archaic Egypt*. London: Penguin Books.

Fairbank, John K. (1990, May 31). From the Ming to Deng Xiaoping. *New York Review of Books*, 16-18.

Fairbank, John King & Goldman, Merle (2006). *China: A new history*. Cambridge, MA: Harvard University Press.

Ferroni, Giulio (1991b). *Storia della letteratura italiana: Dal Cinquecento al Settecento*. Turin: Einaudi Scuola.

Fox, Edward W. (1971). *History in geographic perspective*. New York: W. W. Norton.

Frankfort, Henri (1948). *Kingship and the Gods*.Chicago: University of Chicago Press.

Freeman, Charles (1996). *Egypt, Greece and Rome: Civilizations of the Ancient Mediterranean*.Oxford: Oxford University Press.

Galilei, Galileo (1638/1914). *Dialogue concerning two new sciences*. New York: Macmillan.

Garland, Robert (1992). *Introducing new gods: The politics of Athenian religion*. Ithaca, NY: Cornell University Press.

Geanakoplos, Dennis John (1976). *Interaction of the "sibling" Byzantine and Western culture in The Middle Ages and Italian Renaissance (330-1600)*. New Haven, CT: Yale University Press.

Geymonat, Ludovico (1957). *Galileo Galilei*. Turin: Giulio Einaudi.

Gibbon, Edward (1776-88/1960). *The decline and fall of the Roman Empire*. D.N. Low (abridged). New York: Harcourt, Brace.

Gies, Frances & Joseph (1995). *Cathedral, forge and waterwheel*. New York: HarperPerennial.

Gimpel, Jean (1977). *Medieval machines: The industrial revolution of the Middle Ages*. New York: Penguin.

Godechot, Jacques (1978). Napoleon. In *Encyclopaedia Britannica* (*12*, pp. 831-39). Chicago: Encyclopaedia Britannica.

Goldsworthy, Adrian (2009). *How Rome fell: Death of a superpower*. New Haven, CT: Yale University Press.

Gordon, Benjamin Lee (1959). *Medieval and Renaissance medicine*. New York: Philosophical Library.

Goswami, Amit (1993). An idealist theory of ethics.*Creativity Research Journal*, *6*, 186-96.

Grant, Michael (1975/2000). *The Twelve Caesars.* New York: History Book Club.

Grant, Michael (1998). *From Rome to Byzantium: the fifth century A.D.* London: Routledge.

Griffin, Jasper (1980). *Homer on life and death.* Oxford: Clarendon Press.

Grimal, Nicolas (1992). *A history of ancient Egypt.* London: Blackwell.

Grunebaum, G.E. von (1970). *Classical Islam: A history 600-1258.* Chicago: Aldine Publishers.

Harrison, Lawrence E. (1992). *Who prospers? How cultural values shape economic and political success.* New York: BasicBooks.

Haussig, H.W. (1971). *A history of Byzantine civilization.* New York: Praeger.

Herold, Christopher (1963). *The Age of Napoleon.* New York: American Heritage Publishing.

Herrin, Judith (1987). *The formation of Christendom.* Princeton, NJ: Princeton University Press.

Hong, Fan (1997). *Footbinding, feminism and freedom: the liberation of women's bodies in Modern China.* London: Frank Cass.

Hourani, Albert (1991). *A history of the Arab people.* New York: MJF Books.

James, Thomas Garnet Henry (1978). History of Egypt to the end of the 17th dynasty. In *Encyclopaedia Britannica* (6, pp. 460-71). Chicago: Encyclopaedia Britannica.

Jeal, Tim (-/1989). *Baden-Powell.* London: Hutchinson.

Jeffery, L. H. (1976). *Archaic Greece: The city-states c. 700-500 B.C.* New York: St.Martin's Press.

Jenkins, Romily (1966). *Byzantium: The imperial centuries A.D. 610-1071.* New York: Random House.

Johnson, Paul (1976). *A history of Christianity.* New York: Atheneum.

Kleinman, Arthur & Kleinman, Joan (1991). Suffering and its professional transformation: Toward an ethnography of interpersonal experience. *Culture, Medicine and Psychiatry*, *15*, 275-301.

Köhne, Eckart (2000). Bread and circuses: The politics of entertainment. In E. Köhne and C. Ewigleben (Eds.), *Gladiators and Caesars* (pp. 8-30). Berkeley: University of California Press.

Lane, Frederic C. (1973). *Venice: A maritime republic.* Baltimore, MD: The Johns Hopkins University Press.

Lauritzen, Peter (1978). *Venice: A thousand years of culture and civilization*. London: Weidenfeld and Nicolson.

Lecky, William Edward Hartpole (1869/1955). *History of European morals*. New York: George Braziller.

LeGoff, Jacques (1988). *Medieval civilization 400-1500*. Oxford: Basil Blackwell.

Levy, Howard S. (1966). *Chinese footbinding: The history of a curious erotic custom*. New York: Walton Rawls.

Lewis, Bernard (1947/1993). *The Arabs in history*. Oxford: Oxford University Press.

Lewis, Bernard (2002). *What went wrong? The clash between Islam and Modernity in the Middle East*. New York: HarperCollins.

Lindsay, R. Bruce. (1978). Rome from its Origins to 264 B.C. In *Encyclopaedia Britannica*, (*15*, pp. 1085-91). Chicago: Encyclopaedia Britannica.

Loewe, Michael (1974). *Crisis and Conflict in Han China 104 BC to AD 9*. London: George Allen &Unwin.

Madison, James (1788/2011). The true meaning of the principle of Separation of Powers. In G. Beck & C. Charles (Eds.), *The original argument: The Federalists' case for the Constitution* (pp. 295-306). New York: Threshold Editions.

Mango, Cyril (1980). *Byzantium: The empire of New Rome*. London: Weidenfeld and Nicolson.

Marshall, F.H. & Mavrogordato, John (1949). Byzantine literature. In N.H. Baynes & H.St.L.B. Moss (Eds.) *Byzantium: An introduction to East Roman civilization* (pp. 221-51). Oxford: Clarendon.

Martin Thomas R. (1988, Nov.). Review of R. MacMullen's "Corruption and the Decline of Rome". *History Book Selection*, 7.

Martines, Lauro (2005). *Fire in the city: Savonarola and the struggle for Renaissance Florence*. Oxford: Oxford University Press.

McNeill, William H. (1963). *The rise of the West: A history of the human community*. Chicago: The University of Chicago Press.

McNeill, William H. (1974). *Venice: The hinge of Europe 1081-1797*. Chicago: The University of Chicago Press.

Merson, John (1990). *The genius that was China*. Woodstock, NY: Overlook.

Meyerhof, Max (1931). [Islamic] Science and medicine. In T. Arnold & A. Guillaume (Eds.), *The legacy of Islam* (pp. 311-55). Oxford: Oxford University Press.

Michalopoulos, Andre (1966). *Homer*. Boston: Twayne Publishers.

Miller, Dean A. (1966). *The Byzantine tradition*. New York: Harper & Row.

Mirsky, Jonathan (2001, May 17). Un-Chinese activities (review of J.C. Spence's Treason by the Book), *New York Review of Books,* 38-40.

Mokyr, Joel (1990). *The lever of riches: Technological creativity and economic progress.* New York: Oxford University Press.

Montanelli, Indro, & Gervaso, Roberto (1967). *Italy in the golden centuries*. Chicago: Henry Regnery.

Montesquieu, Baron de (1748/1873). *Spirit of laws*. Cincinnati: Robert Clarke.

Morris, Colin (1972). *The discovery of the individual: 1050-1200.* New York: Harper & Row.

Mote, F. W. (1961). The growth of Chinese despotism: A critique of Wittfogel's theory of Oriental Despotism as applied to China. *Oriens Extremus, 8,* 1-41.

Murphy, Rhoads (1984). City as mirror of society: China, tradition and transformation. In J. A. Agnew, J. Mercer, & D. E. Sopher (Eds.), *The city in cultural context* (pp. 186-204). Boston: Allen &Unwin.

Nasr, SeyyedHossein (1968/1992). *Science and civilization in Islam*. New York: Barnes & Noble.

Needham, Joseph (1985/1998). Introduction. In R. Temple's *The genius of China: 3000 years of science, discovery, and invention* (pp. 6-8). London: Prion.

Nicholl, Charles (2004). *Leonardo da Vinci: Flights of the mind*. New York: Viking.

Nicholson, Reynold A. (1907/1993). *A literary history of the Arabs*. London: Curzon Press.

Nilsson, Martin P. (1980). *A history of Greek religion*. Westport, CT: Greenwood Press.

Nivison, David, S. (1959). "Introduction", "Ho-shen and his accusers". In D.S. Nivison & A.F. Wright (Eds.), *Confucianism in action* (pp. 3-24; 209-43). Stanford, CA: Stanford University Press.

O'Connor, David O. (1983). New Kingdom and Third Intermediate Period. In B.G. Trigger, B.J. Kemp, D. O'Connor, & A. B. Lloyd (Eds.), *Ancient Egypt: A social history* (pp. 183-278). Cambridge: Cambridge University Press.

O'Donnell, T. J. (1967). Castration. In *New Catholic Encyclopaedia* (*3*, p. 194). New York: McGraw Hill.

Petit, Paul (1978).The Later Roman Empire. In *Encyclopaedia Britannica,* (*15*, pp. 1084-1132. Chicago: Encyclopaedia Britannica.

Pirenne, Henri (1925/1969). *Medieval cities: Their origins and the revival of trade.* Princeton: Princeton University Press.

Pollard, John R. T., & Adkins, A. W. H. (2002).Greek religion. In *Encyclopaedia Britannica* (*18*, pp. 784-85). Chicago: Encyclopaedia Britannica.

Popper, Karl R. (1975). *Objective Knowledge.* Oxford: Oxford University Press.

Porter, Roy (1997). *The greatest benefit to mankind: A medical history of humanity.* New York: W. W. Norton.

Prodi, Paolo (1973). The structure and organization of the church in Renaissance Venice. In J. R. Hale (Ed.), *Renaissance Venice* (pp. 409-30). Totowa, NJ: Rowman and Littlefield.

Pye-Smith, Philip H., & Singer, Charles (1973). William Harvey. In *Encyclopaedia Britannica* (*11*, pp. 142-44). Chicago: Encyclopaedia Britannica.

Qadir, C.A. (1988). *Philosophy and science in the Islamic world.* London: Routledge & Kegan Paul.

Rabinowitz, Louis Isaac (1971). Autopsies and dissection. In *Encyclopedia Judaica, (3,* pp. 931-33). Jerusalem: Macmillan.

Rice, David Talbot (1962). *The Byzantines.* London: Thames & Hudson.

Ronan, Colin A. (1983).*The Cambridge illustrated history of the world's science.* New York: Cambridge University Press.

Rowdon, Maurice (1970). *The silver age of Venice.* New York: Praeger.

Runciman, Steven (1956). *Byzantine civilization.* New York: Meridian.

Sakae, Shioya (1956). *Chushingura: An exposition.* Tokyo: Hokuseido Press.

Santillana, Giorgio de (1968/1992). Preface. In S. H. Nasr, *Science and Civilization in Islam* (pp. vii-xiv). New York: Barnes & Noble.

Sapori, Armando (1948/1970). *The Italian merchant on the Middle Ages.* New York: W. W. Norton.

Saunders, J. J. (1965). *A history of Medieval Islam.* London: Routledge and Kegan Paul.

Shirer, William L. (1960). *The rise and fall of the Third Reich.* New York: Simon and Schuster.

Smith, Huston (1998, September 16). Words and things. *New York Review of Books,* 57.

Spence, Jonathan D. (2001). *Treason by the book.* New York: Viking.

Tellenbach, Gerd (1936/1991). *Church, state and Christian society at the time of the Investiture Controversy.* Toronto: University of Toronto Press.

Temple, Robert (1986/1998). *The genius of China: 3000 years of science, discovery, and invention*. London: Prion.

The Book of the thousand nights and one night (-/1986). (Mardus/Mathers translators). London: Routledge.

Thompson, Laurence G. (1978). Chinese religion.In *Encyclopaedia Britannica, (4,* pp. 422-28). Chicago: Encyclopaedia Britannica.

Underwood, E. Ashworth, & Rhodes, Philip (1993). Traditional medicine and surgery in the Orient.In *Encyclopaedia Britannica, (23*, pp. 776-78). Chicago: Encyclopaedia Britannica.

Vidal, Gore (1959/ 1991). Robert Graves and the Twelve Caesars. In J. Gross (Ed.), *The Oxford Book of Essays* (pp. 634-40). Oxford: Oxford University Press.

Wakeman, Frederic Jr. (1975). *The fall of imperial China*. New York: Free Press.

Wallace, Robert (1967). *The World of Leonardo 1452-1519*. New York: Time-Life Books.

Wang Liu, Hui-chen (1959). An analysis of the Chinese clan rules: Confucian theories in action. In D.S. Nivison& A.F. Wright (Eds.). *Confucianism in action* (pp. 63-96). Stanford, CA: Stanford University Press.

Ward, William A. (1965). *The spirit of ancient Egypt.* Beirut: Khayats.

White, Hayden, V. (1966). Introduction. In D.A. Miller, *The Byzantine tradition* (pp. vii-xvi). New York: Harper & Row.

Wills, Garry (2001). *Venice: Lion city — The religion of empire*. New York: Simon & Schuster.

Wilson, John A. (1979). Egyptian civilization. In H. D. Lasswell, H. D. Lerner, H. Speier, (Eds.). *Propaganda and communication in world history, Volume I* (pp. 145-74) Honolulu: The University Press of Hawaii.

Wittfogel, Karl A. (1957). Chinese society: An historical survey. *Journal of Asian Studies, 16,* 343-364.

Woodruff, Winthrop F. (1938). *Roger Bacon: A biography*. London: James Clarke.

Zedler, Beatrice H. (1961). Introduction. In B. H. Zedler (Ed.), *Averroes' "Destruction Destructionum Philosophiae Algazelis"* (pp. 1-53). Milwaukee, WI: Marquette University Press.

Author Index

Adkins, A. W. H. ... 58
Allawi, Ali A. ... 9
Allen, Kerry K. ... 95-96
Anderson, Mary M. ... 19-20
Anderson, William ... 93, 94
Baden-Powell, Robert, S. ... 96
Balazs, Etienne ... 21-22, 23
Baron, Hans ... 71
Beard, Mary ... 66
Beeman, Richard ... 95
Berendt, John ... 50-51
Berlin, Isaiah ... 47n
Bloch, Raymond ... 65-66
Boardman, John ... 56-57
Boorstin, Daniel J. ... 19, 77
Bouwsma, William J. ... 47-48
Breasted, James H ... 60-61, 62-63
Byron, Robert ... 27-28
Cantor, Norman ... 9, 64
Chang, Pang-Mei, Natasha ... 16
Cipolla, Carlo M ... 78, 79, 85-86
Clinton, Bill ... 97n
Commager, Henry Steele ... 95, 97
Crawford, Michael ... 66
Crosby, Alfred W ... 84-85
Dalai Lama, 14th ... 72-73
Dante, Alighieri ... 80n
Dawson, Christopher ... 93
Dennis, George T. ... 28
Diehl, Charles ... 29-30, 31, 32
Dyson, Freeman J. ... 72, 73
Ebrey, Patricia B ... 17
Emery, Walter B. ... 54
Fairbank, John K ... 15, 20
Ferroni, Giulio ... 52
Fox, Edward W ... 55
Frankfort, Henri ... 54-55
Freeman, Charles ... 57, 58, 59
Galilei, Galileo ... 74
Garland, Robert ... 60

Geanakoplos, Dennis John ... 28, 79
Gervaso, Roberto ... 45, 48
Geymonat, Ludovico ... 75
Gibbon, Edward ... 9
Gies, Frances & Joseph ... 75-76
Gimpel, Jean ... 75, 76, 77-78
Godechot, Jacques ... 70n
Goldman, Merle ... 15, 20
Goldsworthy, Adrian ... 70-71
Gordon, Benjamin Lee ... 87
Goswami, Amit ... 96
Grant, Michael ... 29, 69, 70
Griffin, Jasper ... 59-60
Grimal, Nicolas ... 61
Grunebaum, G.E. von ... 41-42
Harrison, Lawrence E. ... 24
Haussig, H.W. ... 27
Herold, Christopher ... 70n
Herrin, Judith ... 73-74
Hong, Fan ... 16
Hourani, Albert ... 33n
James, Thomas Garnet Henry ... 53, 62
Jeal, Tim ... 96
Jeffery, L. H. ... 57
Jenkins, Romily ... 30
Johnson, Paul ... 92
King, Martin Luther ... 97n
Kleinman, Arthur ... 13
Kleinman, Joan ... 13
Köhne, Eckart ... 67
Lane, Frederic C. ... 49, 51
Lauritzen, Peter ... 50
Lecky, William Edward Hartpole ... 67-68
LeGoff, Jacques ... 83-84
Levy, Howard S ... 14, 17
Lewis, Bernard ... 9, 36-37, 37n
Lindsay, R. Bruce ... 66
Loewe, Michael ... 18
Madison, James ... 95
Mango, Cyril ... 27, 29

Marshall, F.H. 9
Martin Thomas R. 68-69
Martines, Lauro 9
Mavrogordato, John 9
McNeill, William H 26, 43, 45, 45-46,
            51, 52, 53, 55, 68, 82-83
Merson, John 80-81, 83
Meyerhof, Max 33, 42, 87
Michalopoulos, Andre 59
Miller, Dean A 31, 32
Mirsky, Jonathan 23n
Mokyr, Joel 9, 11, 12, 21, 80, 81
Montanelli, Indro 45, 48
Montesquieu, Baron de 94
Morris, Colin 84
Mote, F. W. 20, 22
Murphy, Rhoads 80
Nasr, Seyyed Hossein 34-35, 35-36, 42
Needham, Joseph 11, 63, 82
Nicholl, Charles… 88
Nicholson, Reynold A 40
Nilsson, Martin P. 59
Nivison, David, S 19, 21
O'Connor, David O… 62
O'Donnell, T. J 18
Petit, Paul 64-65, 66-67
Pirenne, Henri 47
Pollard, John R. T 58
Popper, Karl R 90
Porter, Roy 86-87
Prodi, Paolo 46-47
Pye-Smith, Philip H. 90-91

Qadir, C.A. 34
Rabinowitz, Louis Isaac 86-87
Rhodes, Philip 86
Rice, David Talbot 30
Ronan, Colin A 33-34
Rowdon, Maurice 48-49, 51-52
Runciman, Steven 31
Santillana, Giorgio de 43
Sapori, Armando 37-38
Saunders, J. J 33n, 35, 38n, 39-40, 42
Shirer, William L. 92
Singer, Charles 90-91
Smith, Huston… 72
Spence, Jonathan D. 23n
Tellenbach, Gerd 46
Temple, Robert 11-12, 83
*The Book of the thousand nights and
one night* 37, 38-39
Thompson, Laurence G 82
Underwood, E. 86
Vidal, Gore 69-70
Wakeman, Frederic 23-24
Wallace, Robert 88-89
Wang Liu, Hui-chen 17n
Ward, William A. 54
White, Hayden, V. 25n, 30-31
Wills, Garry 47, 49-50
Wilson, John A. 61-62
Wittfogel, Karl A. 22
Woodruff, Winthrop F. 75
Zedler, Beatrice H 41

Subject Index

Age of Translation.................. 36, 38n
Alexander III, Pope.................. 74
Al-Ghazzali.................. 42-43
Anatomia Mundini.................. 87-88
Arab World.................. 9, 33-43
Averroes.................. 41
Bacon, Roger.................. 75
Baden-Powell.................. 96
Benedictine monks.................. 75-77
Bread and games.................. 67-68
Byzantium.................. 9, 26-32, 47, 50, 73-74, 77-79, 85, 87
Cambridge, 1174.................. 77n
Canossa, 1077.................. 74, 85, 97n
Castration.................. 18
cesarismo veneziano.................. 46
Ch'ing emperors.................. 20-21, 24
Charlemagne.................. 38n
China.................. 9, 11-25, 80-83
Chushingura.................. 24-25
Cistercian monks.................. 75-77
Dante.................. 92, 93-94
Dante's clock.................. 80, 80n
Democratic clock.................. 77
Dissections (public).................. 86-89
Division of Power (DP).................. 30, 35-39, 85, 91-92, 97
DP Greece.................. 63
DP Learning.................. 35-41, 60
DP origins of science.................. 72-89
DP Polytheism.................. 58-60
DP Tuscans.................. 71
Dream of the Red Chambers.................. 25
Dunant, Henri.................. 91
Egypt.................. 53-63
Eunuchism.................. 18-20
Federalist.................. 95
Footbinding.................. 14-18
fox ideas.................. 47-48
fox thinkers.................. 47n

Frederick I, Barbarossa.................. 74, 80
Führerprinzip.................. 92
Galen.................. 87
Gladiators.................. 67
Greece.................. 9, 53-63
Greek Orthodox Church.................. 77-78
Greek seas.................. 55-58
Gregory VII, Pope.................. 46, 74
Happiness.................. 96-97
Harun al-Rashid.................. 38n
Harvey, William.................. 90-91
Henry IV, Emperor.................. 46, 74
Hitler, Adolf.................. 92
Homeric "DP Bible".................. 59-60
Hsükuang-han.................. 18
Human body's discovery.................. 86-89
Humbert of Silva Candida.................. 93
Imperial panegyrics.................. 28
Individualism.................. 84
insular ethonpsychology.................. 29
insular scripts.................. 28
insulars.................. 13, 13n, 29, 42
Investiture Controversy.................. 32, 46, 93
Japan.................. 24-25
King, Martin Luther.................. 97n
Leonardo's dissections.................. 88-89
Lord Acton's dictum.................. 69
Madison, James.................. 95
Mandarins.................. 23
Mechanization.................. 85-86
Mein Kampf.................. 92
Ming emperors.................. 80-81
Monarchia.................. 93-95
Mondino de Luzzi.................. 87-89
Montesquieu.................. 92, 94-95
Napoleon.................. 70n
Nile.................. 53
Objective knowledge.................. 90
Pax Islamica.................. 34
Peregrinus, Peter.................. 75

Subject Index ♦ 109

Peter the Great..............................51
Plymouth Rock, 1620.....................97n
Quantification............................84-85
quasi-visitor 13, 42
Quing emperors.........................80-81
Red Cross......................................91
Rome.....................................9, 64-71
Runnymede, 1215 ....97n
Sarpi, Paolo...............................46-47
Sindbad the Merchant 37-39
SPQR...65
Ssu-Ma Ch'ien 19
Tagore, Rabindranath 96
Truth..90-91
Twelve Caesars 69-70

Unity of Power (UP)............. 30-32, 39-43, 45-46, 91-92
UP Egypt.......................................63
UP Polytheism..........................54-55
Venice....................................9, 44-52
Vesalius, Andrea......................87, 89
Visitors 13, 13n
Volunteering as DP...................95-97
war of scripts..........................49-50
War of Supremacy....................83-84
Waterwheels.............................75-76
Western Church.......................77-80
Western Science......................72-80
Western World.....................9, 79-89